REPORT FROM
IRON MOUNTAIN

REPORT FROM
IRON
MOUNTAIN

ON THE POSSIBILITY AND
DESIRABILITY OF PEACE

by

LEONARD C. LEWIN

WITH AN INTRODUCTION BY VICTOR NAVASKY

THE FREE PRESS

NEW YORK   LONDON   TORONTO   SYDNEY   TOKYO   SINGAPORE

THE FREE PRESS
A Division of Simon & Schuster, Inc.
1230 Avenue of the Americas
New York, N.Y. 10020

The Free Press and colophon are trademarks
of Simon & Schuster Inc.

Designed by Michael Mendelsohn of MM Design 2000, Inc.

Manufactured in the United States of America

printing number
10 9 8 7 6 5 4 3 2 1

Victor Navasky is copyright holder of the new introduction

Library of Congress Cataloging-in-Publication Data

Lewin, Leonard C.
    Report from Iron Mountain : on the possibility and desirability of
peace/ by Leonard C. Lewin : with an introd. by Victor Navasky.
        p.   cm.

    ISBN-13: 978-1-439-12311-9
    ISBN-10: 1-439-12311-X

    1. Peace.   2. Economic conversion—United States.   3. Economic
conversion.   4. Literary forgeries and mystifications.   I. Title.
JX1963.R46   1996
355.02—dc20   96–555
                                                                      CIP

CONTENTS

CONTENTS

INTRODUCTION

BY VICTOR NAVASKY

IN SPRING OF 1995 the *Wall Street Journal* ran a front-page story on *Report From Iron Mountain*, a book that the Michigan Militia and other far-right groups regarded as a "sort of bible"—along with *The Turner Diaries* and Pat Robertson's *New World Order.*

The Turner Diaries is a fantasy of right-wing revolution and the *New World Order* an expose, with antisemitic undertones, of how a cabal of international bankers runs the world. But *Report From Iron Mountain*, which purports to be a suppressed government report, is—as the *Journal* reported—a 1967 hoax perpetrated by writer Leonard Lewin.

In fact it was far more than a hoax; it was a satire, a parody, a provocation. Its acceptance by super-patriots and conspiracy theorists of the far right is roughly akin to the Irish Republican Army considering Jonathan Swift's *A Modest Proposal* proof that eating babies is official British policy.

The militia connection is only the latest chapter in the bizarre career of an idea that became a surprise best seller. The idea: Put the unpopular subject of conversion from a military to peacetime economy on the national agenda. Since I was present at the creation, let me try to explain.

In the late 1950s and early 1960s I was editor and publisher of a magazine of political satire called *Monocle*, which was born at Yale Law School as "a leisurely quarterly of political satire" (that meant we came out twice a year), but it eventually graduated, along with the rest of us. Although we later published one—and only one—issue as what we called a "monthly," by the mid-sixties we called ourselves "a radical sporadical," which meant that we came out like the United Nations police force—only in emergencies and only when we could meet our financial obligations.

Our official line was that "the views of our contributors, no matter how conflicting and contradictory, are the views of the editors."

Unofficially, we were mostly left-liberal Democrats with anarcho-syndicalist pretensions. Typically, we ran the Gettysburg address in Eisenhowerese by Oliver Jensen ("I haven't checked these figures yet, but eighty-seven years ago I think it was . . ."); when J.F.K. failed to integrate publicly assisted housing with "a stroke of the presidential pen," as he had promised he would, we started the Ink for Jack campaign, urging our subscribers to deluge the White House with bottles of ink; and we even launched a comic strip with a peacenik-hero who said the magic equation and turned into a fat superman who looked suspiciously like the Hudson Institute's Herman Kahn.

For several years we managed to defy George S. Kaufman's adage that "satire is what closes on Saturday night," but our last regular number appeared in 1965. By that time, however, our subscription price was "Ten issues for $7.50, or $5 for a lifetime subscription." So in a metaphysical sense one might say that we are still in business, and this new edition of *Report From Iron Mountain* is, in a way, evidence that we are.

When *Monocle* ran out of money, as we saw it we had two choices: We could do the honorable thing, and in the great tradition of American capitalism declare bankruptcy, go into Chapter 11, and pay our creditors one cent on the dollar. Or, in the jargon of the early sixties, we could sell out. In fact, before we went out of the magazine business we ran a symposium where we asked one hundred celebrities to fill out a one-question questionnaire: "Why I Sold Out," which is what we did, or tried to do.

We could write our personal books on our own time but, in line with the non-book fashion of the day, pay our debts to society and our creditors from un-books. The basic idea was to come up with bestselling book ideas, or rather non-book ideas, that required researchers rather than writers, and find trade book publishers willing to pay for and publish them. Then we'd hire researchers to research them and split the vast profits among all concerned. Since the idea was to make money and some of our best, i.e., worst, ideas were calculated to appeal to the largest possible audience, i.e., the lowest common denominator, we not only had no pride of authorship, we had shame of authorship, preferring to play an anonymous, behind-the-scenes role. In that capacity we were responsible for over thirty un-books on none of which did we put our name. Now it can be told that although they were published under such imprints as Simon & Schuster, Bantam Books, Putnam, Workman, and so forth, *Monocle* was the real perpetrator behind such classics as *The Beatles, Words Without Music* (transcripts of Beatles press conferences), *Barbed Wires,* a collection of famous funny telegrams (Did you know that when Robert Benchley arrived in Venice he sent a telegram saying, STREETS FULL OF WATER, PLEASE ADVISE?), *The Illustrated Gift Edition of The Communist Manifesto* (the cover blurb was "'Revolutionary!' V. I. Lenin"), *The Algonquin Wits,* dictionaries such as *Drugs from A to Z,* and so forth.

But as it turned out we were unsuited to follow the simple formula we had invented: Have other people research books based on clichéd ideas that would appeal to the masses, while we clipped coupons. Call it hubris, call it boredom, or call it incompetence, I prefer to think that our instincts were insufficiently base. For instance, when a lawyer-friend told us that Delacorte Publishing had sold on supermarket counters alone more than two million copies of a little, 25-cent chap book called *A Wife's Rights*, our immediate thought was to produce a quickie on *Kid's Rights*. But the researcher we recruited claimed that it was impossible and perhaps even unethical to reduce the complexities of children's rights to horn-book law one-liners. She persuaded us that the subject called for a real book and proceeded to research and write it, under the snappy title *Up Against the Law*. Of course it received respectful reviews and instead of selling in the millions, it sold in the tens of thousands.

Weary of non-books and wary of real books, we missed the opportunity *Monocle* had afforded to comment on the passing scene. And there was much on which to comment. Those were the days of the Vietnam war when our military and political leaders kept assuring us that there was "light at the end of the tunnel," that our boys "will be home by Christmas." With Grove Press as publisher, we did put out an entire book of quotations by L.B.J., General Westmoreland, and lesser evils predicting the imminent end of the war. Needless to say, the war—and the predictions—continued long after this particular un-book was published.

That book may have been a turning point for us, however. We continued to spawn collections, anthologies, and other ephemera but somehow they got more and more serious (dare I say distinguished?) and sold fewer and fewer copies. Under our aegis, James Boylan, the former editor of the *Columbia Journalism Review*, put together a thoroughly scholarly, annotated selection of articles from what was arguably the best newspaper this country ever produced, the old *New York World*. Two Berkeley grad students collected the most interesting essays written about the free speech movement and what followed, under the title *Revolution at Berkeley*, and Irving Howe wrote a smart and prescient introduction that anticipated the campus turmoils to come in the early seventies.

It was in that context that *Report From Iron Mountain: On the Possibility and Desirability of Peace* was born. The year was 1966 and one morning the *New York Times* featured a short news item about how the stock market had tumbled because of what the headline called a "Peace Scare."

The news item had no byline, but it seemed to those of us around the editors' table in the *Monocle* office worthy of Jonathan Swift, H. L. Mencken, Mark Twain. Around the table, in addition to myself were Marvin Kitman and Richard Lingeman. Kitman, our news managing editor, had been *Monocle*'s candidate for president in 1964. He ran in the Republican primary against Barry Goldwater as what he called "a Lincoln Republican." Unlike Goldwater, whose platform only went back to McKinley, Kitman claimed to be the only real conservative because his platform went back one hundred years and called for unconditional surrender of the South, freeing the slaves and the reinforcement of the garrison at Fort Sumter. Lingeman, *Monocle*'s executive editor, had served as Kitman's "holy ghostwriter," and eventually moved on to a distinguished career as Theodore Dreiser's and now Sinclair Lewis's biographer and is my colleague at *The Nation*.

We, of course, naively believed that the prospect of peace would be as welcome on Wall Street as in *Monocle*'s low-rent Greenwich Village offices. All of which got us thinking. Suppose the government had appointed a task force to plan the transition from a wartime economy and the task force concluded that we couldn't afford it because our entire economy was based on the preparation for war and without this threat it would collapse? The report therefore was suppressed.

In the spirit of Mencken's famous hoax about the introduction of the bathtub to the U.S. (he claimed that only after Millard Fillmore introduced one into the White House did Americans, who previously regarded them as unsanitary, start to bathe regularly), we decided to publish the story of the suppression of this report.

To give the book credibility we needed an ultra-respectable mainstream publisher, but one with a sense of humor and the pluck to pull off a hoax. This publisher should also share our belief in the importance of putting the subject of economic conversion from a military to a peacetime economy on the national agenda.

Luckily for us the ideal candidate was at hand. Our collection of essays growing out of the free speech movement at Berkeley had been published by Dial Press, whose list included such prestigious writers as James Baldwin, Norman Mailer, and Richard Condon. As a result we came to know Dial's maverick publisher, Richard Baron, and its imaginative editor-in-chief, author of a little-known novel called *Welcome to Hard Times*, one E. L. Doctorow, who subsequently came to fame as the author of *The Book of Daniel*, *Ragtime*, and other novels that seemed dedicated to the proposition that fiction could be a path to deeper truths than non-fiction. Sight unseen, they signed on and proposed listing the book in their catalogue as non-fiction, and not even telling their salesman about the hoax.

We had equal luck with our choice of author. We knew that Leonard Lewin, who had edited an anthology of political satire (under the pseudonym of L. L. Case), was a student of the genre. We knew that he cared passionately about issues of war and peace. And his wicked simultaneous parody of the historian Arthur Schlesinger, Jr., and Eisenhower speechwriter Emmet Hughes's memoir, *The Ordeal of Power*, which *Monocle* magazine had published under Lewin's title "The Ordeal of Rhetoric," showed him to be a sophisticated observer of what Ike had called in his farewell speech (written with the help of Hughes), the military-industrial complex.

There was only one problem. Lewin insisted that he couldn't write the story of the suppression of the so-called report, until there was a report to be suppressed. And so, with the discreet input of his *Monocle* colleagues and folks ranging from Arthur Waskow, then at The Institute for Policy Studies in Washington (who was at work on what he called "A History of the Future"); W. H. Ferry of The Center for the Study of Democratic Institutions in Santa Barbara, California; John Kenneth Galbraith, who was back at Harvard after his stint as JFK's Ambassador to India; and a small cadre of *Monocle* interns to track down original sources, Lewin wrote the report. Titled *Report From Iron Mountain: On the Possibility and Desirability of Peace*, it was a brilliant imitation of think-tankese rendered in impenetrable, bureaucratic prose, replete with obfuscating footnotes, all of them, except for two trick ones, to real if esoteric sources, in a variety of languages.

When we read the report, we all agreed that it had to be published in its entirety. Thus the report became the body of the book and the narrative of its suppression became what appears in the pages that follow as "Foreword," "Background Information," and "Statement by John Doe."

As it happened, our carefully planned cover story (or "legend" as they say in the C.I.A.) paid off. When John Leo, then a reporter for the *New York Times*, spotted the non-fiction listing of the Report in Dial's catalogue, he made the traditional round of calls to determine whether it was real or a hoax. At Dial he was told if he thought it was a fraud he should check the footnotes, virtually all of which, of course, checked out. No advance reviewer in the trade publications had been willing to label it a hoax, and the State Department's Arms Control and Disarmament Agency carefully said, "To our knowledge no such special study group ever existed." When he called the White House, instead of a denial, Leo got a no-comment—we'll have-to-check-it-out-but-don't-quote-us. (For all the L.B.J. White House knew, the J.F.K. White House *had* commissioned such a study.) The upshot was that the *Times* ran Leo's story saying that the possible hoax was a possibly suppressed report on the front page. The headline, which itself could have been a parody of *Times* style, said "Some see book as hoax/Others take it seriously."

Then, John Kenneth Galbraith, who had been writing a series of spoof articles for *Esquire* under the pseudonym Mark Epernay about a fictitious "psychometrist," Professor Herschel McLandress (creator of the McLandress Dimension, a theory about how long people can go without thinking about themselves—e.g., Henry Kissinger achieved a coefficient of 6.0 minutes on the scale), wrote a review in *Book World* under the name of McLandress. The professor concluded, "As I would put my personal repute behind the authenticity of this document, so I would testify to the validity of its conclusions. My reservations relate only to the wisdom of releasing it to an obviously unconditioned public." The review led to speculation that Galbraith himself had written *Report From Iron Mountain*. He called a press conference to deny he had anything to do with it. There were only two conceivable authors, he said: Dean Rusk or Clare Boothe Luce.

A number of people—most of them in government and

regular readers of bureaucratese—came to believe the *Report* was the real thing. Some reviewers praised it as a satire. *Transaction* magazine devoted the better part of an issue to a sober discussion of the questions the *Report* raised. The symposiasts, in addition to editor-in-chief Irving Louis Horowitz, included Kenneth Boulding, Herb Gans, and other distinguished policy-intellectuals. Most interesting were the reactions of Herman Kahn and Henry Kissinger, who took the satire personally and angrily dismissed it as sophomoric and idiotic, and Fletcher Prouty, a national security aide in the Kennedy Administration (the model for the Donald Sutherland character in Oliver Stone's *JFK*) who said he believed it was the real McCoy. In 1972 Lewin confessed his authorship in the *New York Times Book Review*. He had intended, he wrote, "to caricature the bankruptcy of the think-tank mentality by pursuing its style of scientistic thinking to its logical ends." He defended the hoax technique as the best way to gain attention for the book and its underlying message.

In a weird coda, Lewin discovered in the mid-1980s that the ultraright Liberty Lobby and others believing that the report was a government document, had disseminated thousands of copies without bothering to request permission and some of these copies were being sold through Liberty Lobby's hate-filled newspaper, *The Spotlight*. He sued and the case was settled out of court, resulting in the withdrawal of thousands of copies of the bootleg edition, which now reside in Lewin's living room. But well-worn copies continued to circulate along with a six-hour video based on the book.

One might have thought that the hoax, having been confessed, proclaimed, and even adjudicated, would, after twenty-five years, have been laid to rest. But no, like a radioactive substance, it seemed to have a half-life of its own. On May 9, 1995, the *Wall Street Journal* ran a front page story headlined:

> *A Cause for Fear*
> Though Called a Hoax
> 'Iron Mountain' Report
> Guides Some Militias

Iron Mountain, it seemed, had returned. And now, to the loonies in the boonies, here was evidence of a government plot so sinister it would make Waco look like a panty raid. *Aux arms, citoyens!*

So why won't *Iron Mountain* go away? Perhaps it's partly because pied piper Lewin, with his perfect pitch, has stumbled on a netherworld for paranoids—the black hole of government secrecy and deception, where Kennedy assassinationologists today march in lockstep with white supremacists, neo-Nazis, and militiamen. By exposing their exaggerated fears and suspicions, he also taps into our own unresolved political conflicts.

But make no mistake about it. The contradictions in contemporary culture are not confined to paranoids. These days anti-interventionist alumni of the peace movement have found themselves on the same "side" as isolationists like Pat Buchanan in opposing U.S. intervention in Bosnia. Ditto civil libertarians and NRA activists in opposing measures like 1995's so-called counter-terrorism bill. *Iron Mountain* speaks to a moment when it is unclear whether such convergences mean political realignment or simply signify confusion.

Given *Report From Iron Mountain*'s twisted trajectory, one hesitates to draw any "conclusions" from this tale. Here, however, are some interim reflections:

The cold war may be over, but the bloated military

budget that undergirds *Iron Mountain*'s premise isn't. When last heard from, the U.S. Senate had approved a $265.3 billion defense bill—$7.5 billion more than the Pentagon and the President had asked for.

Paranoid conspiracy theorists now believe that the quashing of the *Iron Mountain* report is itself a real government conspiracy because they are paranoid and conspiracy theorists. But their perspective can only be reinforced by the refusal of the government and particularly our intelligence agencies to release millions of still-classified documents, some of these pre–cold war relics dating back more than fifty years.

For libertarians, who occupy that weird 1990s limbo where left meets right in their joint distrust of The State, *Iron Mountain* confirms their belief that too often claims of national security are a cloak for government lies, cover-ups, and bureaucratic disinformation.

Indeed, the *faux* neutrality of *Iron Mountain*'s narrative voice seems to have had the ironic effect of permitting a broad spectrum of constituencies to read their own meanings into Leonard Lewin's text. In this way it may be said to have separate but equal resonance for military Keynesians who might see it as an "irresponsible"? "sophomoric"? satire and members of the Michigan militia and other groups who might draw on it for a different sort of ammunition.

Lewin's skillful parody of think-tankese, the language of ponderous objectivity, and think-tank-think, which emphasizes a "value-free" approach to issues of great moral moment, underlines the folly of confusing moderation of tone with credibility and of assigning so-called value neutrality a sacrosanct place in public discourse.

The *Report* was a success in that it achieved its mission, which in this case was to provoke thinking about the unthinkable—the conversion to a peacetime economy and the absurdity of the arms race. But it was a failure, given that even with the end of the cold war we still have a cold war economy (which makes the *Report* all the more relevant today).

The *Report* also raised the perennial question of reality outdistancing satire. As Lewin later wrote, "The Pentagon Papers were not written by someone like me. Neither was the Defense Department's *Pax Americana* study (how to take over Latin America)."

Finally, the fact that today's ultraright conspiracy theorists, reinforced in their paranoia by governmental abuse and secrecy, take Lewin's scenario as seriously as the think-tankers take themselves is, of course, the scariest proposition of all. Every time Lewin or others in on the hoax confess, the conspiracy theorists regard it as further proof of a cover-up.

When I wrote about this phenomenon in *The Nation* I said that perhaps the only way to put a stop to this speculation is to tell them: "Guys, you're right! *Report From Iron Mountain* is a real document. Remember: You read it here in the pro-Commie, pro-government, pro-Jewish, anti-American *Nation*."

But the sad truth may be that the jargonized prose, worst-case scenario thinking, and military value-laden assumptions that Lewin so artfully skewers are still with us. And if that is true, the joke is not on the Michigan and other militias. It is on the rest of us, and it's no longer so funny.

Victor Navasky
November 1995

REPORT FROM
IRON MOUNTAIN

FOREWORD

"JOHN DOE," as I will call him in this book for reasons that will be made clear, is a professor at a large university in the Middle West. His field is one of the social sciences, but I will not identify him beyond this. He telephoned me one evening last winter, quite unexpectedly; we had not been in touch for several years. He was in New York for a few days, he said, and there was something important he wanted to discuss with me. He wouldn't say what it was. We met for lunch the next day at a midtown restaurant.

He was obviously disturbed. He made small talk for half an hour, which was quite out of character, and I didn't press him. Then, apropos of nothing, he mentioned a dispute between a writer and a prominent political family that had been in the headlines. What, he wanted to know, were my views on "freedom of information"? How would I qualify them? And so on. My answers were not memorable, but they seemed to satisfy him. Then, quite abruptly, he began to tell me the following story:

Early in August of 1963, he said, he found a message on his desk that a "Mrs. Potts" had called him from Washington. When he returned the call, a *man* answered immediately, and told Doe, among other things, that he had been selected to serve on a commission "of the highest importance." Its objective was *to determine, accurately and realistically, the nature of the problems that would confront the United States if and when a condition of "permanent peace" should arrive, and to draft a program for dealing with this contingency.* The man described the unique procedures that

1

were to govern the commission's work and that were expected to extend its scope far beyond that of any previous examination of these problems.

Considering that the caller did not precisely identify either himself or his agency, his persuasiveness must have been of a truly remarkable order. Doe entertained no serious doubts of the *bona fides* of the project, however, chiefly because of his previous experience with the excessive secrecy that often surrounds quasi-governmental activities. In addition, the man at the other end of the line demonstrated an impressively complete and surprisingly detailed knowledge of Doe's work and personal life. He also mentioned the names of others who were to serve with the group; most of them were known to Doe by reputation. Doe agreed to take the assignment—he felt he had no real choice in the matter—and to appear the second Saturday following at Iron Mountain, New York. An airline ticket arrived in his mail the next morning.

The cloak-and-dagger tone of this convocation was further enhanced by the meeting place itself. Iron Mountain, located near the town of Hudson, is like something out of Ian Fleming or E. Phillips Oppenheim. It is an underground nuclear hideout for hundreds of large American corporations. Most of them use it as an emergency storage vault for important documents. But a number of them maintain substitute corporate headquarters as well, where essential personnel could presumably survive and continue to work after an attack. This latter group includes such firms as Standard Oil of New Jersey, Manufacturers Hanover Trust, and Shell.

I will leave most of the story of the operations of the Special Study Group, as the commission was formally called, for Doe to tell in his own words ("Background

Information"). At this point it is necessary to say only that it met and worked regularly for over two and a half years, after which it produced a Report. It was this document, and what to do about it, that Doe wanted to talk to me about.

The Report, he said, had been suppressed—both by the Special Study Group itself and by the government inter-agency committee to which it had been submitted. After months of agonizing, Doe had decided that he would no longer be party to keeping it secret. What he wanted from me was advice and assistance in having it published. He gave me his copy to read, with the express understanding that if for any reason I were unwilling to become involved, I would say nothing about it to anyone else.

I read the Report that same night. I will pass over my own reactions to it, except to say that the unwillingness of Doe's associates to publicize their findings became readily understandable. What had happened was that they had been so tenacious in their determination to deal *comprehensively* with the many problems of transition to peace that the original questions asked of them were never quite answered. Instead, this is what they concluded:

Lasting peace, while not theoretically impossible, is probably unattainable; even if it could be achieved it would almost certainly not be in the best interests of a stable society to achieve it.

That is the gist of what they say. Behind their qualified academic language runs this general argument: War fills certain functions essential to the stability of our society; until other ways of filling them are developed, the war system must be maintained—and improved in effectiveness.

It is not surprising that the Group, in its Letter of Transmittal, did not choose to justify its work to "the lay reader, unexposed to the exigencies of higher political or military responsibility." Its Report was addressed, deliberately, to unnamed government administrators of high rank; it assumed considerable political sophistication from this select audience. To the general reader, therefore, the substance of the document may be even more unsettling than its conclusions. He may not be prepared for some of its assumptions—for instance, that most medical advances are viewed more as problems than as progress; or that poverty is necessary and desirable, public postures by politicians to the contrary notwithstanding; or that standing armies are, among other things, social-welfare institutions in exactly the same sense as are old-people's homes and mental hospitals. It may strike him as odd to find the probable explanation of "flying saucer" incidents disposed of *en passant* in less than a sentence. He may be less surprised to find that the space program and the "controversial" antimissile missile and fallout shelter programs are understood to have the spending of vast sums of money, not the advancement of science or national defense, as their principal goals, and to learn that "military" draft policies are only remotely concerned with defense.

He may be offended to find the organized repression of minority groups, and even the reestablishment of slavery, seriously (and on the whole favorably) discussed as possible aspects of a world at peace. He is not likely to take kindly to the notion of the *deliberate* intensification of air and water pollution (as part of a program leading to peace), even when the reason for considering it is made clear. That a world without war will have to turn sooner rather than later to universal test-tube procreation will be less disturbing, if no more appealing. But few readers will not be taken aback, at least, by a few lines in the Report's conclusions, repeated in its formal recommendations, that suggest that the long-range planning—and "budgeting"— of the "optimum" number of lives to be destroyed annually in overt warfare is high on the Group's list of priorities for government action.

I cite these few examples primarily to warn the general reader what he can expect. The statesmen and strategists for whose eyes the Report was intended obviously need no such protective admonition.

This book, of course, is evidence of my response to Doe's request. After carefully considering the problems that might confront the publisher of the Report, we took it to The Dial Press. There, its significance was immediately recognized, and, more important, we were given firm assurances that no outside pressures of any sort would be permitted to interfere with its publication.

It should be made clear that Doe does not disagree with the substance of the Report, which represents a genuine consensus in all important respects. He constituted a minority of one—but only on the issue of disclosing it to the general public. A look at how the Group dealt with *this* question will be illuminating.

The debate took place at the Group's last full meeting before the Report was written, late in March, 1966, and again at Iron Mountain. Two facts must be kept in mind, by way of background. The first is that the Special Study Group had never been explicitly charged with or sworn to secrecy, either when it was convened or at any time thereafter. The second is that the Group had nevertheless operated *as if* it had been. This was assumed from the circumstances of its inception and from the tone of its instructions.

(The Group's acknowledgment of help from "the many persons ... who contributed so greatly to our work" is somewhat equivocal; these persons were not told the nature of the project for which their special resources of information were solicited.)

Those who argued the case for keeping the Report secret were admittedly motivated by fear of the explosive political effects that could be expected from publicity. For evidence, they pointed to the suppression of the far less controversial report of then-Senator Hubert Humphrey's subcommittee on disarmament in 1962. (Subcommittee members had reportedly feared that it might be used by Communist propagandists, as Senator Stuart Symington put it, to "back up the Marxian theory that war production was the reason for the success of capitalism.") Similar political precautions had been taken with the better-known Gaither Report in 1957, and even with the so-called Moynihan Report in 1965.

Furthermore, they insisted, a distinction must be made between serious studies, which are normally classified unless and until policy makers decide to release them, and conventional "showcase" projects, organized to demonstrate a political leadership's concern about an issue and to deflect the energy of those pressing for action on it. (The example used, because some of the Group had participated in it, was a "White House Conference" on international cooperation, disarmament, etc., which had been staged late in 1965 to offset complaints about escalation of the Vietnam war.)

Doe acknowledges this distinction, as well as the strong possibility of public misunderstanding. But he feels that if the sponsoring agency had wanted to *mandate* secrecy it could have done so at the outset. It could also have assigned the project to one of the government's established "think tanks," which normally work on a classified basis. He scoffed at fear of public reaction, which could have no lasting effect on long-range measures that might be taken to implement the Group's proposals, and derided the Group's abdication of responsibility for its opinions and conclusions. So far as he was concerned, there was such a thing as a public *right* to know what was being done on its behalf; the burden of proof was on those who would abridge it.

If my account seems to give Doe the better of the argument, despite his failure to convince his colleagues, so be it. My participation in this book testifies that I am not neutral. In my opinion, the decision of the Special Study Group to censor its own findings was not merely timid but presumptuous. But the refusal, as of this writing, of the agencies for which the Report was prepared to release it themselves raises broader questions of public policy. Such questions center on the continuing use of self-serving definitions of "security" to avoid possible political embarrassment. It is ironic how often this practice backfires.

I should state, for the record, that I do not share the attitudes toward war and peace, life and death, and survival of the species manifested in the Report. Few readers will. In human terms, it is an outrageous document. But it does represent a serious and challenging effort to define an enormous problem. And it explains, or certainly appears to explain, aspects of American policy otherwise incomprehensible by the ordinary standards of common sense. What we may think of these explanations is something else, but it seems to me that we are entitled to know not only what they are but whose they are.

By "whose" I don't mean merely the names of the authors of the Report. Much more important, we have a right to know to what extent their assumptions of social necessity are shared by the decision-makers in our government. Which do they accept and which do they reject? However disturbing the answers, only full and frank discussion offers any conceivable hope of solving the problems raised by the Special Study Group in their Report from Iron Mountain.

L.C.L.
New York, June 1967

BACKGROUND
INFORMATION

[*The following account of the workings of the Special Study Group is taken verbatim from a series of tape-recorded interviews I had with "John Doe." The transcript has been edited to minimize the intrusion of my questions and comments, as well as for length, and the sequence has been revised in the interest of continuity.* L.C.L.]

How was the Group formed?

. . . The general idea for it, for this kind of study, dates back at least to 1961. It started with some of the new people who came in with the Kennedy administration, mostly, I think, with McNamara, Bundy, and Rusk. They were impatient about many things. . . . One of them was that no really serious work had been done about planning for peace—a long-range peace, that is, with long-range planning.

Everything that had been written on the subject [before 1961] was superficial. There was insufficient appreciation of the scope of the problem. The main reason for this, of course, was that the idea of a real peace in the world, general disarmament and so on, was looked on as utopian. Or even crackpot. This is still true, and it's easy enough to understand when you look at what's going on in the world today. . . . It was reflected in the studies that had been made up to that time. They were not realistic. . . .

The idea of the Special Study, the exact form it would take, was worked out early in '63. . . . The settlement of the Cuban missile affair had something to do with it, but what

9

helped most to get it moving were the big changes in military spending that were being planned. . . . Plants being closed, relocations, and so forth. Most of it wasn't made public until much later. . . .

[I understand] it took a long time to select the people for the Group. The calls didn't go out until the summer. . . .

Who made the selection?

That's something I can't tell you. I wasn't involved with the preliminary planning. The first I knew of it was when I was called myself. But three of the people had been in on it, and what the rest of us know we learned from them, about what went on earlier. I do know that it started very informally. I don't know what particular government agency approved the project.

Would you care to make a guess?

All right—I think it was an *ad hoc* committee, at the cabinet level, or near it. It had to be. I suppose they gave the organizational job—making arrangements, paying the bills, and so on—to somebody from State or Defense or the National Security Council. Only one of us was in touch with Washington, and I wasn't the one. But, I can tell you that very, very few people knew about us. . . . For instance, there was the Ackley Committee.[1] It was set up *after* we were. If you read their report—the same old tune—economic reconversion, turning sword plants into plowshare factories—I think you'll wonder if even the President

---

[1] This was a "Committee on the Economic Impact of Defense and Disarmament," headed by Gardner Ackley, of the Council of Economic Advisers. It was established by Presidential order in December, 1963, and issued a report in July, 1965.

knew about our Group. The Ackley Committee certainly didn't.

Is that possible, really? I mean that not even the President knew of your commission?

Well, I don't think there's anything odd about the government attacking a problem at two different levels. Or even about two or three [government] agencies working at cross-purposes. It happens all the time. Perhaps the President did know. And I don't mean to denigrate the Ackley Committee, but it was exactly that *narrowness* of approach that we were supposed to get away from. . . .

You have to remember—you've read the Report—that what they wanted from us was a different kind of *thinking*. It was a matter of approach. Herman Kahn calls it "Byzantine"—no agonizing over cultural and religious values. No moral posturing. It's the kind of thinking that Rand and the Hudson Institute and I.D.A.[2] brought into *war* planning. . . . What they asked us to do, and I think we did it, was to give the same kind of treatment to the hypothetical problems of peace as they give to a hypothetical nuclear war. . . . We may have gone further than they expected, but once you establish your premises and your logic you can't turn back. . . .

Kahn's books,[3] for example, are misunderstood, at least by laymen. They shock people. But you see, what's important about them is not his conclusions, or his opinions. It's the *method*. He has done more than anyone else I can think of to get the general public accustomed to the *style* of modern military thinking. . . . Today it's possible for a columnist to write about "counterforce strategy" and "minimum

[2] The Institute for Defense Analysis.

[3] *On Thermonuclear War, Thinking About the Unthinkable, On Escalation.*

deterrence" and "credible first-strike capability" without having to explain every other word. He can write about war and strategy without getting bogged down in questions of morality. . . .

The other big difference about our work is breadth. The Report speaks for itself. I can't say that we took *every* relevant aspect of life and society into account, but I don't think we missed anything essential. . . .

Why was the project given to an outside commission? Why couldn't it have been handled directly by an appropriate government agency?

I think that's obvious, or should be. The kind of thinking wanted from our Group just isn't to be had in a formal government operation. Too many constraints. Too many inhibitions. This isn't a new problem. Why else would outfits like Rand and Hudson stay in business? Any assignment that's at all sophisticated is almost always given to an outside group. This is true even in the State Department, in the "gray" operations, those that are supposed to be unofficial, but are really as official as can be. Also with the C.I.A. . . .

For our study, even the private research centers were too institutional. . . . A lot of thought went into making sure that *our* thinking would be unrestricted. All kinds of little things. The way we were called into the Group, the places we met, all kinds of subtle devices to remind us. For instance, even our name, the Special Study Group. You know government names. Wouldn't you think we'd have been called "Operation Olive Branch," or "Project Pacifica," or something like that? Nothing like that for us—too allusive, too suggestive. And no minutes of our meetings—too inhibiting. . . . About who might be reading them. Of course, we took notes for our own use. And among ourselves, we usually called ourselves "The Iron Mountain Boys," or "Our Thing," or whatever came to mind. . . .

What can you tell me about the members of the Group?

I'll have to stick to generalities. . . . There were fifteen of us. The important thing was that we represented a very wide range of disciplines. And not all academic. People from the natural sciences, the social sciences, even the humanities. We had a lawyer and a businessman. Also, a professional war planner. Also, you should know that everyone in the Group had done work of distinction in at least two different fields. The interdisciplinary element was built in. . . .

It's true that there were no women in the Group, but I don't think that was significant. . . . We were all American citizens, of course. And all, I can say, in very good health, at least when we began. . . . You see, the first order of business, at the first meeting, was the reading of dossiers. They were very detailed, and not just professional, but also personal. They included medical histories. I remember one very curious thing, for whatever it's worth. Most of us, and that includes me, had a record of abnormally high uric acid concentrations in the blood. . . . None of us had ever had this experience, of a public inspection of credentials, or medical reports. It was very disturbing. . . .

But it was deliberate. The reason for it was to emphasize that we were supposed to make *all* our own decisions on procedure, without outside rules. This included judging each other's qualifications and making allowances for possible bias. I don't think it affected our work directly, but it made the point it was supposed to make. . . . That we should ignore absolutely nothing that might conceivably affect our objectivity.

[At this point I persuaded Doe that a brief occupational description of the individual members of the Group would serve a useful purpose for readers of the Report. The list which follows was worked out on paper. (It might be more accurate to say it was negotiated.) The problem was to give as much relevant information as possible without violating Doe's commitment to protect his colleagues' anonymity. It turned out to be very difficult, especially in the cases of those members who are very well known. For this reason, secondary areas of achievement or reputation are usually not shown.

The simple alphabetical "names" were assigned by Doe for convenient reference; they bear no intended relation to actual names. "Able" was the Group's Washington contact. It was he who brought and read the dossiers, and who most often acted as chairman. He, "Baker," and "Cox" were the three who had been involved in the preliminary planning. There is no other significance to the order of listing.

"Arthus Able" is an historian and political theorist, who has served in government.

"Bernard Baker" is a professor of international law and a consultant on government operations.

"Charles Cox" is an economist, social critic, and biographer.

"John Doe."

"Edward Ellis" is a sociologist often involved in public affairs.

"Frank Fox" is a cultural anthropologist.

"George Green" is a psychologist, educator, and developer of personnel testing systems.

"Harold Hill" is a psychiatrist, who has conducted extensive studies of the relationship between individual and group behavior.

"John Jones" is a scholar and literary critic.

"Martin Miller" is a physical chemist, whose work has received international recognition at the highest level.

"Paul Peters" is a biochemist, who has made important discoveries bearing on reproductive processes.

"Richard Roe" is a mathematician affiliated with an independent West Coast research institution.

"Samuel Smith" is an astronomer, physicist, and communications theorist.

"Thomas Taylor" is a systems analyst and war planner, who has written extensively on war, peace, and international relations.

"William White" is an industrialist, who has undertaken many special government assignments.]

How did the Group operate? I mean, where and when did you meet, and so forth?

We met on the average of once a month. Usually it was on weekends, and usually for two days. We had a few longer sessions, and one that lasted only four hours. . . . We met all over the country, always at a different place, except for the first and last times, which were at Iron Mountain. It was like a traveling seminar. . . . Sometimes at hotels, sometimes at universities. Twice we met at summer camps, and once at a private estate, in Virginia. We used a business place in Pittsburgh, and another in Poughkeepsie [New York]. . . . We never met in Washington, or on government property anywhere. . . . Able would announce the times and places two meetings ahead. They were never changed. . . .

We didn't divide into subcommittees, or anything else that formal. But we all took individual assignments between meetings. A lot of it involved getting information from other people. . . . Among the fifteen of us, I don't think there was anybody in the academic or professional world we couldn't call on if we wanted to, and we took advantage of it. . . . We were paid a very modest per diem. All of it was called "expenses" on the vouchers. We were told not to report it on our tax returns. . . . The checks were drawn on a special account of Able's at a New York bank. He signed them. . . . I don't know what the study cost. So far as our time and travel were concerned, it couldn't have come to more than the low six-figure range. But the big item must have been computer time, and I have no idea how high this ran. . . .

You say that you don't think your work was affected by professional bias. What about political and philosophical bias? Is it possible to deal with questions of war and peace without reflecting personal values?

Yes, it is. I can understand your skepticism. But if you had been at any of our meetings you'd have had a very hard time figuring out who were the liberals and who were the conservatives, or who were hawks and who were doves. There *is* such a thing as objectivity, and I think we had it. . . . I don't say no one had any emotional reaction to what we were doing. We all did, to some extent. As a matter of fact, two members had heart attacks after we were finished, and I'll be the first to admit it probably wasn't a coincidence.

You said you made your own ground rules. What were these ground rules?

The most important were informality and unanimity. By informality I mean that our discussions were open-ended. We went as far afield as any one of us thought we had to. For instance, we spent a lot of time on the relationship between military recruitment policies and industrial employment. Before we were finished with it, we'd gone through the history of western penal codes and any number of comparative psychiatric studies [of draftees and volunteers]. We looked over the organization of the Inca empire. We determined the effects of automation on underdeveloped societies. . . . It was all relevant. . . .

By unanimity, I don't mean that we kept taking votes, like a jury. I mean that we stayed with every issue until we had what the Quakers call a "sense of the meeting." It was time-consuming. But in the long run it saved time. Eventually we all got on the same wavelength, so to speak. . . .

Of course we had differences, and big ones, especially in the beginning. . . . For instance, in Section 1 you might think we were merely clarifying our instructions. Not so; it took a long time before we all agreed to a strict interpretation. . . . Roe and Taylor deserve most of the credit for this. . . . There are many things in the Report that look obvious now, but didn't seem so obvious then. For instance, on the relationship of war to social systems. The original premise was conventional, from Clausewitz. . . .

That war was an "instrument" of broader political values. Able was the only one who challenged this, at first. Fox called his position "perverse." Yet it was Fox who furnished most of the data that led us all to agree with Able eventually. I mention this because I think it's a good example of the way we worked. A triumph of method over cliché. . . . I certainly don't intend to go into details about who took what side about what, and when. But I will say, to give credit where due, that only Roe, Able, Hill, and Taylor were able to see, at the beginning, where our method was taking us.

But you always reached agreement, eventually.
      Yes. It's a unanimous report. . . . I don't mean that our sessions were always harmonious. Some of them were rough. The last six months there was a lot of quibbling about small points. . . . We'd been under pressure for a long time, we'd been working together too long. It was natural . . . that we got on each other's nerves. For a while Able and Taylor weren't speaking to each other. Miller threatened to quit. But this all passed. There were no important differences. . . .

How was the Report actually written? Who did the writing?
      We all had a hand in the first draft. Jones and Able put it together, and then mailed it around for review before working out a final version. . . . The only problems were the form it should take and whom we were writing it for. And, of course, the question of disclosure. . . . [Doe's comments on this point are summarized in the introduction.]

You mentioned a "peace games" manual. What are peace games?

I wanted to say something about that. The Report barely mentions it. "Peace games" is a method we developed during the course of the study. It's a forecasting technique, an information system. I'm very excited about it. Even if nothing is done about our recommendations—which is conceivable—this is something that can't be ignored. It will revolutionize the study of social problems. It's a by-product of the study. We needed a fast, dependable procedure to approximate the effects of disparate social phenomena on other social phenomena. We got it. It's in a primitive phase, but it works.

How are peace games played? Are they like Rand's war games?

You don't "play" peace games, like chess or Monopoly, any more than you play war games with toy soldiers. You use computers. It's a programming system. A computer "language," like Fortran, or Algol, or Jovial. . . . Its advantage is its superior capacity to interrelate data with no apparent common points of reference. . . . A simple analogy is likely to be misleading. But I can give you some examples. For instance, supposing I asked you to figure out what effect a moon landing by U.S. astronauts would have on an election in, say, Sweden. Or what effect a change in the draft law—a specific change—would have on the value of real estate in downtown Manhattan? Or a certain change in college entrance requirements in the United States on the British shipping industry?

You would probably say, first, that there would be no effect to speak of, and second, that there would be no way of telling. But you'd be wrong on both counts. In each case there would be an effect, and the peace games method could tell you what it would be, quantitatively. I didn't take these examples out of the air. We used them in working out the method. . . . Essentially, it's an elaborate high-speed trial-and-error system for determining working algorithms. Like most sophisticated types of computer problem-solving. . . .

A lot of the "games" of this kind you read about are just glorified conversational exercises. They really are games, and nothing more. I just saw one reported in the Canadian Computer Society Bulletin, called a "Vietnam Peace Game." They use simulation techniques, but the programming hypotheses are speculative. . . .

The idea of a problem-solving system like this is not original with us. ARPA[4] has been working on something like it. So has General Electric, in California. There are others. . . . We were successful not because we know more than they do about programming, which we don't, but because we learned how to formulate the problems accurately. It goes back to the old saw. You can always find the answer if you know the right question. . . .

Supposing you hadn't developed this method. Would you have come to the same conclusions in the Report?

Certainly. But it would have taken many times longer. . . . But please don't misunderstand my enthusiasm [about the peace games method]. With all due respect to the effects of computer technology on modern thinking, basic judgments must still be made by human beings. The peace games technique isn't responsible for our Report. We are. . . .

[4] The Advanced Research Projects Agency, of the Department of Defense.

STATEMENT BY "JOHN DOE"

CONTRARY TO THE DECISION of the Special Study Group, of which I was a member, I have arranged for the general release of our Report. I am grateful to Mr. Leonard C. Lewin for his invaluable assistance in making this possible, and to The Dial Press for accepting the challenge of publication. Responsibility for taking this step, however, is mine and mine alone.

I am well aware that my action may be taken as a breach of faith by some of my former colleagues. But in my view my responsibility to the society of which I am a part supersedes any self-assumed obligation on the part of fifteen individual men. Since our Report can be considered on its merits, it is not necessary for me to disclose their identity to accomplish my purpose. Yet I would gladly abandon my own anonymity if it were possible to do so without at the same time compromising theirs, to defend our work publicly if and when they release me from this personal bond.

But this is secondary. What is needed now, and needed badly, is widespread public discussion and debate about the elements of war and the problems of peace. I hope that publication of this Report will serve to initiate it.

THE REPORT OF THE
SPECIAL STUDY GROUP

LETTER OF TRANSMITTAL

TO THE CONVENER OF THIS GROUP:

Attached is the Report of the Special Study Group established by you in August, 1963, 1) to consider the problems involved in the contingency of a transition to a general condition of peace, and 2) to recommend procedures for dealing with this contingency. For the convenience of nontechnical readers we have elected to submit our statistical supporting data, totaling 604 exhibits, separately, as well as a preliminary manual of the "peace games" method devised during the course of our study.

We have completed our assignment to the best of our ability, subject to the limitations of time and resources available to us. Our conclusions of fact and our recommendations are unanimous; those of us who differ in certain secondary respects from the findings set forth herein do not consider these differences sufficient to warrant the filing of a minority report. It is our earnest hope that the fruits of our deliberations will be of value to our government in its efforts to provide leadership to the nation in solving the complex and far-reaching problems we have examined, and that our recommendations for subsequent Presidential action in this area will be adopted.

Because of the unusual circumstances surrounding the establishment of this Group, and in view of the nature of its findings, we do not recommend that this Report be released for publication. It is our affirmative judgment that such action would not be in the public interest. The uncertain advantages of public discussion of our conclusions and recommendations are, in our opinion, greatly outweighed by the clear and predictable danger of a crisis in public confidence which untimely publication of this Report might be expected to provoke. The likelihood that a lay reader, unexposed to the exigencies of higher political or military responsibility, will misconstrue the purpose of this project, and the intent of its participants, seems obvious. We urge that circulation of this Report be closely restricted to those whose responsibilities require that they be apprised of its contents.

We deeply regret that the necessity of anonymity, a prerequisite to our Group's unhindered pursuit of its objectives, precludes proper acknowledgment of our gratitude to the many persons in and out of government who contributed so greatly to our work.

For the Special Study Group
[*signature withheld for publication*]

30 September, 1966

INTRODUCTION

THE REPORT WHICH FOLLOWS summarizes the results of a two-and-a-half-year study of the broad problems to be anticipated in the event of a general transformation of American society to a condition lacking its most critical current characteristics: its capability and readiness to make war when doing so is judged necessary or desirable by its political leadership.

Our work has been predicated on the belief that some kind of general peace may soon be negotiable. The *de facto* admission of Communist China into the United Nations now appears to be only a few years away at most. It has become increasingly manifest that conflicts of American national interest with those of China and the Soviet Union are susceptible of political solution, despite the superficial contraindications of the current Vietnam war, of the threats of an attack on China, and of the necessarily hostile tenor of day-to-day foreign policy statements. It is also obvious that differences involving other nations can be readily resolved by the three great powers whenever they arrive at a stable peace among themselves. It is not necessary, for the purposes of our study, to assume that a general détente of this sort *will* come about—and we make no such argument—but only that it *may*.

It is surely no exaggeration to say that a condition of general world peace would lead to changes in the social structures of the nations of the world of unparalleled and revolutionary magnitude. The economic impact of general disarmament, to name only the most obvious consequence of peace, would revise the production and distribution patterns of the globe to a degree that would make the changes of the past fifty years seem insignificant. Political, sociological, cultural, and ecological changes would be equally far-reaching. What has motivated our study of these contingencies has been the growing sense of thoughtful men in and out of government that the world is totally unprepared to meet the demands of such a situation.

We had originally planned, when our study was initiated, to address ourselves to these two broad questions and their components: *What can be expected if peace comes? What should we be prepared to do about it?* But as our investigation proceeded it became apparent that certain other questions had to be faced. What, for instance, are the real functions of war in modern societies, beyond the ostensible ones of defending and advancing the "national interests" of nations? In the absence of war, what other institutions exist or might be devised to fulfill these functions? Granting that a "peaceful" settlement of disputes is within the range of current international relationships, is the abolition of war, in the broad sense, really possible? If so, is it necessarily desirable, in terms of social stability? If not, what can be done to improve the operation of our social system in respect to its war-readiness?

The word *peace,* as we have used it in the following pages, describes a permanent, or quasi-permanent, condition entirely free from the national exercise, or contemplation, of any form of the organized social violence, or threat of violence, generally known as war. It implies total and general disarmament. It is not used to describe the more familiar condition of "cold war," "armed peace," or other mere respite, long or short, from armed conflict. Nor is it used simply as a synonym for the political settlement of international differences. The magnitude of modern means of mass destruction and the speed of modern communications require the unqualified working definition given above; only a generation ago such an absolute description would have seemed utopian rather than pragmatic. Today, any modification of this definition would render it almost worthless for our purpose. By the same standard, we have used the word *war* to apply interchangeably to conventional ("hot") war, to the general condition of war preparation or war readiness, and to the general "war system." The sense intended is made clear in context.

The first section of our Report deals with its scope and with the assumptions on which our study was based. The second considers the effects of disarmament on the economy, the subject of most peace research to date. The third takes up so-called "disarmament scenarios" which have been proposed. The fourth, fifth, and sixth examine the nonmilitary functions of war and the problems they raise for a viable transition to peace; here will be found some indications of the true dimensions of the problem, not previously coordinated in any other study. In the seventh section we summarize our findings, and in the eighth we set forth our recommendations for what we believe to be a practical and necessary course of action.

SCOPE OF THE STUDY

W HEN THE SPECIAL STUDY GROUP was established in
August, 1963, its members were instructed to govern their deliberations in accordance with three principal
criteria. Briefly stated, they were these: 1) military-style
objectivity; 2) avoidance of preconceived value assumptions; 3) inclusion of all relevant areas of theory and data.

These guideposts are by no means as obvious as they
may appear at first glance, and we believe it necessary to
indicate clearly how they were to inform our work. For
they express succinctly the limitations of previous "peace
studies," and imply the nature of both government and
unofficial dissatisfaction with these earlier efforts. It is not
our intention here to minimize the significance of the work
of our predecessors, or to belittle the quality of their con-
tributions. What we have tried to do, and believe we have
done, is extend their scope. We hope that our conclusions
may serve in turn as a starting point for still broader and
more detailed examinations of every aspect of the problems of transition to peace and of the questions which
must be answered before such a transition can be allowed
to get under way.

It is a truism that objectivity is more often an intention
expressed than an attitude achieved, but the intention—
conscious, unambiguous, and constantly self-critical—is a
precondition to its achievement. We believe it no accident
that we were charged to use a "military contingency"

model for our study, and we owe a considerable debt to the civilian war planning agencies for their pioneering work in the objective examination of the contingencies of nuclear war. There is no such precedent in peace studies. Much of the usefulness of even the most elaborate and carefully reasoned programs for economic conversion to peace, for example, has been vitiated by a wishful eagerness to demonstrate that peace is not only possible, but even cheap or easy. One official report is replete with references to the critical role of "dynamic optimism" on economic developments, and goes on to submit, as evidence, that it "would be hard to imagine that the American people would not respond very positively to an agreed and safeguarded program to substitute an international rule of law and order," etc.[1] Another line of argument frequently taken is that disarmament would entail comparatively little disruption of the economy, since it need only be partial; we will deal with this approach later. Yet genuine objectivity in war studies is often criticized as inhuman. As Herman Kahn, the writer on strategic studies best known to the general public, put it: "Critics frequently object to the icy rationality of the Hudson Institute, the Rand Corporation, and other such organizations. I'm always tempted to ask in reply, 'Would you prefer a warm, human error? Do you feel better with a nice emotional mistake?'"[2] And, as Secretary of Defense Robert S. McNamara has pointed out, in reference to facing up to the possibility of nuclear war, "Some people are afraid even to look over the edge. But in a thermonuclear war we cannot afford any political acrophobia."[3] Surely it should be self-evident that this applies equally to the opposite prospect, but so far no one has taken more than a timid glance over the brink of peace.

An intention to avoid preconceived value judgments is

if anything even more productive of self-delusion. We claim no immunity, as individuals, from this type of bias, but we have made a continuously self-conscious effort to deal with the problems of peace without, for example, considering that a condition of peace is *per se* "good" or "bad." This has not been easy, but it has been obligatory; to our knowledge, it has not been done before. Previous studies have taken the desirability of peace, the importance of human life, the superiority of democratic institutions, the greatest "good" for the greatest number, the "dignity" of the individual, the desirability of maximum health and longevity, and other such wishful premises as axiomatic values necessary for the justification of a study of peace issues. We have not found them so. We have attempted to apply the standards of physical science to our thinking, the principal characteristic of which is not quantification, as is popularly believed, but that, in Whitehead's words, ". . . it ignores all judgments of value; for instance, all esthetic and moral judgments."[4] Yet it is obvious that any serious investigation of a problem, however "pure," must be informed by some normative standard. In this case it has been simply the survival of human society in general, of American society in particular, and, as a corollary to survival, the stability of this society.

It is interesting, we believe, to note that the most dispassionate planners of nuclear strategy also recognize that the stability of society is the one bedrock value that *cannot* be avoided. Secretary McNamara has defended the need for American nuclear superiority on the grounds that it "makes possible a strategy designed to preserve the fabric of our societies if war should occur."[5] A former member of the Department of State policy planning staff goes further. "A more precise word for peace, in terms of the practical world, is stability. . . . Today the great nuclear panoplies are essential elements in such stability as exists. Our present purpose must be to continue the process of learning how to live with them."[6] We, of course, do not equate stability with peace, but we accept it as the one common assumed objective of both peace and war.

The third criterion—breadth—has taken us still farther afield from peace studies made to date. It is obvious to any layman that the economic patterns of a warless world will be drastically different from those we live with today, and it is equally obvious that the political relationships of nations will not be those we have learned to take for granted, sometimes described as a global version of the adversary system of our common law. But the social implications of peace extend far beyond its putative effects on national economies and international relations. As we shall show, the relevance of peace and war to the internal political organization of societies, to the sociological relationships of their members, to psychological motivations, to ecological processes, and to cultural values is equally profound. More important, it is equally critical in assaying the consequences of a transition to peace, and in determining the feasibility of any transition at all.

It is not surprising that these less obvious factors have been generally ignored in peace research. They have not lent themselves to systematic analysis. They have been difficult, perhaps impossible, to measure with any degree of assurance that estimates of their effects could be depended on. They are "intangibles," but only in the sense that abstract concepts in mathematics are intangible compared to those which can be quantified. Economic factors, on the other hand, can be measured, at least superficially; and international relationships can be verbalized, like law, into logical sequences.

We do not claim that we have discovered an infallible way of measuring these other factors, or of assigning them precise weights in the equation of transition. But we believe we have taken their relative importance into account to this extent: we have removed them from the category of the "intangible," hence scientifically suspect and therefore somehow of secondary importance, and brought them out into the realm of the objective. The result, we believe, provides a context of realism for the discussion of the issues relating to the possible transition to peace which up to now has been missing.

This is not to say that we presume to have found the answers we were seeking. But we believe that our emphasis on breadth of scope has made it at least possible to begin to understand the questions.

DISARMAMENT AND THE ECONOMY

I N THIS SECTION we shall briefly examine some of the common features of the studies that have been published dealing with one or another aspect of the expected impact of disarmament on the American economy. Whether disarmament is considered as a by-product of peace or as its precondition, its effect on the national economy will in either case be the most immediately felt of its consequences. The quasi-mensurable quality of economic manifestations has given rise to more detailed speculation in this area than in any other.

General agreement prevails in respect to the more important economic problems that general disarmament would raise. A short survey of these problems, rather than a detailed critique of their comparative significance, is sufficient for our purposes in this Report.

The first factor is that of size. The "world war industry," as one writer[1] has aptly called it, accounts for approximately a tenth of the output of the world's total economy. Although this figure is subject to fluctuation, the causes of which are themselves subject to regional variation, it tends to hold fairly steady. The United States, as the world's richest nation, not only accounts for the largest single share of this expense, currently upward of $60 billion a year, but also ". . . has devoted a higher *proportion* [emphasis added] of its gross national product to its military establishment than any other major free world nation. This was true even before our increased expenditures in Southeast Asia."[2] Plans for economic conversion that minimize the economic magnitude of the problem do so only by rationalizing, however persuasively, the maintenance of a substantial residual military budget under some euphemized classification.

Conversion of military expenditures to other purposes entails a number of difficulties. The most serious stems from the degree of rigid specialization that characterizes modern war production, best exemplified in nuclear and missile technology. This constituted no fundamental problem after World War II, nor did the question of free-market consumer demand for "conventional" items of consumption—those goods and services consumers had already been conditioned to require. Today's situation is qualitatively different in both respects.

This inflexibility is geographical and occupational, as well as industrial, a fact which has led most analysts of the economic impact of disarmament to focus their attention on phased plans for the relocation of war industry personnel and capital installations as much as on proposals for developing new patterns of consumption. One serious flaw common to such plans is the kind called in the natural sciences the "macroscopic error." An implicit presumption is made that a total national plan for conversion differs from a community program to cope with the shutting down of a "defense facility" only in degree. We find no reason to believe that this is the case, nor that a general enlargement of such local programs, however well thought out in terms of housing, occupational retraining, and the like, can be applied on a national scale. A national economy can absorb almost any number of subsidiary reorganizations within its total limits, providing there is no basic change in its own structure. General disarmament, which would require such basic changes, lends itself to no valid smaller-scale analogy.

Even more questionable are the models proposed for the retraining of labor for nonarmaments occupations. Putting aside for the moment the unsolved questions dealing with the nature of new distribution patterns—retraining for what?—the increasingly specialized job skills associated with war industry production are further depreciated by the accelerating inroads of the industrial techniques loosely described as "automation." It is not too much to say that general disarmament would require the scrapping of a critical proportion of the most highly developed occupational specialties in the economy. The political difficulties inherent in such an "adjustment" would make the outcries resulting from the closing of a few obsolete military and naval installations in 1964 sound like a whisper.

In general, discussions of the problems of conversion have been characterized by an unwillingness to recognize its special quality. This is best exemplified by the 1965 report of the Ackley Committee.[3] One critic has tellingly pointed out that it blindly assumes that ". . . nothing in the arms economy—neither its size, nor its geographical concentration, nor its highly specialized nature, nor the peculiarities of its market, nor the special nature of much of its labor force—endows it with any uniqueness when the necessary time of adjustment comes."[4]

Let us assume, however, despite the lack of evidence

that a viable program for conversion can be developed in the framework of the existing economy, that the problems noted above can be solved. What proposals have been offered for utilizing the productive capabilities that disarmament would presumably release?

The most commonly held theory is simply that general economic reinvestment would absorb the greater part of these capabilities. Even though it is now largely taken for granted (and even by today's equivalent of traditional laissez-faire economists) that unprecedented government assistance (and concomitant government control) will be needed to solve the "structural" problems of transition, a general attitude of confidence prevails that new consumption patterns will take up the slack. What is less clear is the nature of these patterns.

One school of economists has it that these patterns will develop on their own. It envisages the equivalent of the arms budget being returned, under careful control, to the consumer, in the form of tax cuts. Another, recognizing the undeniable need for increased "consumption" in what is generally considered the public sector of the economy, stresses vastly increased government spending in such areas of national concern as health, education, mass transportation, low-cost housing, water supply, control of the physical environment, and, stated generally, "poverty."

The mechanisms proposed for controlling the transition to an arms-free economy are also traditional—changes in both sides of the federal budget, manipulation of interest rates, etc. We acknowledge the undeniable value of fiscal tools in a normal cyclical economy, where they provide leverage to accelerate or brake an existing trend. Their more committed proponents, however, tend to lose sight of the fact that there is a limit to the power of these devices to influence fundamental economic forces. They can provide new incentives in the economy, but they cannot in themselves transform the production of a billion dollars' worth of missiles a year to the equivalent in food, clothing, prefabricated houses, or television sets. At bottom, they reflect the economy; they do not motivate it.

More sophisticated, and less sanguine, analysts contemplate the diversion of the arms budget to a nonmilitary system equally remote from the market economy. What the "pyramid-builders" frequently suggest is the expansion of space-research programs to the dollar level of current armaments expenditures. This approach has the superficial merit of reducing the size of the problem of transferability of resources, but introduces other difficulties, which we will take up in section 6.

Without singling out any one of the several major studies of the expected impact of disarmament on the economy for special criticism, we can summarize our objections to them in general terms as follows:

1. No proposed program for economic conversion to disarmament sufficiently takes into account the unique magnitude of the required adjustments it would entail.

2. Proposals to transform arms production into a beneficent scheme of public works are more the products of wishful thinking than of realistic understanding of the limits of our existing economic system.

3. Fiscal and monetary measures are inadequate as controls for the process of transition to an arms-free economy.

4. Insufficient attention has been paid to the political acceptability of the objectives of the proposed conversion models, as well as of the political means to be employed in effectuating a transition.

5. No serious consideration has been given, in any pro-

posed conversion plan, to the fundamental nonmilitary function of war and armaments in modern society, nor has any explicit attempt been made to devise a viable substitute for it. This criticism will be developed in sections 5 and 6.

DISARMAMENT SCENARIOS

S CENARIOS, as they have come to be called, are hypothetical constructions of future events. Inevitably, they are composed of varying proportions of established fact, reasonable inference, and more or less inspired guesswork. Those which have been suggested as model procedures for effectuating international arms control and eventual disarmament are necessarily imaginative, although closely reasoned; in this respect they resemble the "war games" analyses of the Rand Corporation, with which they share a common conceptual origin.

All such scenarios that have been seriously put forth imply a dependence on bilateral or multilateral agreement between the great powers. In general, they call for a progressive phasing out of gross armaments, military forces, weapons, and weapons technology, coordinated with elaborate matching procedures of verification, inspection, and machinery for the settlement of international disputes. It should be noted that even proponents of unilateral disarmament qualify their proposals with an implied requirement of reciprocity, very much in the manner of a scenario of graduated response in nuclear war. The advantage of unilateral initiative lies in its political value as an expression of good faith, as well as in its diplomatic function as a catalyst for formal disarmament negotiations.

The READ model for disarmament (developed by the Research Program on Economic Adjustments to Disarmament) is typical of these scenarios. It is a twelve-year program, divided into three-year stages. Each stage includes a separate phase of: reduction of armed forces; cutbacks of weapons production, inventories, and foreign military bases; development of international inspection procedures and control conventions; and the building up of a sovereign international disarmament organization. It anticipates a net matching decline in U.S. defense expenditures of only somewhat more than half the 1965 level, but a necessary redeployment of some five-sixths of the defense-dependent labor force.

The economic implications assigned by their authors to various disarmament scenarios diverge widely. The more conservative models, like that cited above, emphasize economic as well as military prudence in postulating elaborate fail-safe disarmament agencies, which themselves require expenditures substantially substituting for those of the displaced war industries. Such programs stress the advantages of the smaller economic adjustment entailed.[1] Others emphasize, on the contrary, the magnitude (and the opposite advantages) of the savings to be achieved from disarmament. One widely read analysis[2] estimates the annual cost of the inspection function of general disarmament throughout the world as only between two and three percent of current military expenditures. Both types of plan tend to deal with the anticipated problem of economic reinvestment only in the aggregate. We have seen no proposed disarmament sequence that correlates the phasing out of specific kinds of military spending with specific new forms of substitute spending.

Without examining disarmament scenarios in greater detail, we may characterize them with these general comments:

1. Given genuine agreement of intent among the great powers, the scheduling of arms control and elimination presents no inherently insurmountable procedural problems. Any of several proposed sequences might serve as the basis for multilateral agreement or for the first step in unilateral arms reduction.

2. No major power can proceed with such a program, however, until it has developed an economic conversion plan fully integrated with each phase of disarmament. No such plan has yet been developed in the United States.

3. Furthermore, disarmament scenarios, like proposals for economic conversion, make no allowance for the non-military functions of war in modern societies, and offer no surrogate for these necessary functions. One partial exception is a proposal for the "unarmed forces of the United States," which we will consider in section 6.

WAR AND PEACE
AS SOCIAL SYSTEMS

W e have dealt only sketchily with proposed disarmament scenarios and economic analyses, but the reason for our seemingly casual dismissal of so much serious and sophisticated work lies in no disrespect for its competence. It is rather a question of relevance. To put it plainly, all these programs, however detailed and well developed, are abstractions. The most carefully reasoned disarmament sequence inevitably reads more like the rules of a game or a classroom exercise in logic than like a prognosis of real events in the real world. This is as true of today's complex proposals as it was of the Abbé de St. Pierre's "Plan for Perpetual Peace in Europe" 250 years ago.

Some essential element has clearly been lacking in all these schemes. One of our first tasks was to try to bring this missing quality into definable focus, and we believe we have succeeded in doing so. We find that at the heart of every peace study we have examined—from the modest technological proposal (e.g., to convert a poison gas plant to the production of "socially useful" equivalents) to the most elaborate scenario for universal peace in our time— lies one common fundamental misconception. It is the source of the miasma of unreality surrounding such plans. *It is the incorrect assumption that war, as an institution, is subordinate to the social systems it is believed to serve.*

This misconception, although profound and far-reaching, is entirely comprehensible. Few social clichés are so unquestioningly accepted as the notion that war is an extension of diplomacy (or of politics, or of the pursuit of economic objectives). If this were true, it would be wholly appropriate for economists and political theorists to look on the problems of transition to peace as essentially mechanical or procedural—as indeed they do, treating them as logistic corollaries of the settlement of national conflicts of interest. If this were true, there would be no real substance to the difficulties of transition. For it is evident that even in today's world there exists no conceivable conflict of interest, real or imaginary, between nations or between social forces within nations, that cannot be resolved without recourse to war—*if* such resolution were assigned a priority of social value. And if this were true, the economic analyses and disarmament proposals we have referred to, plausible and well conceived as they may be, would not inspire, as they do, an inescapable sense of indirection.

The point is that the cliché is not true, and the problems of transition are indeed substantive rather than merely procedural. Although war is "used" as an instrument of national and social policy, the fact that a society is organized for any degree of readiness for war supersedes its political and economic structure. War itself is the basic social system, within which other secondary modes of social organization conflict or conspire. It is the system which has governed most human societies of record, as it is today.

Once this is correctly understood, the true magnitude of the problems entailed in a transition to peace—itself a social system, but without precedent except in a few simple preindustrial societies—becomes apparent. At the same time, some of the puzzling superficial contradictions of modern societies can then be readily rationalized. The "unnecessary" size and power of the world war industry; the preeminence of the military establishment in every society, whether open or concealed; the exemption of military or paramilitary institutions from the accepted social and legal standards of behavior required elsewhere in the society; the successful operation of the armed forces and the armaments producers entirely outside the framework of each nation's economic ground rules: these and other ambiguities closely associated with the relationship of war to society are easily clarified, once the priority of war-making potential as the principal structuring force in society is accepted. Economic systems, political philosophies, and corpora jures serve and extend the war system, not vice versa.

It must be emphasized that the precedence of a society's war-making potential over its other characteristics is not the result of the "threat" presumed to exist at any one time from other societies. This is the reverse of the basic situation; "threats" against the "national interest" are usually created or accelerated to meet the changing needs of the war system. Only in comparatively recent times has it been considered politically expedient to euphemize war budgets as "defense" requirements. The necessity for governments to distinguish between "aggression" (bad) and "defense" (good) has been a by-product of rising literacy and rapid communication. The distinction is tactical only, a concession to the growing inadequacy of ancient war-organizing political rationales.

Wars are not "caused" by international conflicts of interest. Proper logical sequence would make it more often accurate to say that war-making societies require—and thus bring about—such conflicts. The capacity of a nation to make war expresses the greatest social power it can exercise; war-making, active or contemplated, is a matter of life and death on the greatest scale subject to social control. It should therefore hardly be surprising that the military institutions in each society claim its highest priorities.

We find further that most of the confusion surrounding the myth that war-making is a tool of state policy stems from a general misapprehension of the functions of war. In general, these are conceived as: to defend a nation from military attack by another, or to deter such an attack; to defend or advance a "national interest"—economic, political, ideological; to maintain or increase a nation's military power for its own sake. These are the visible, or ostensible, functions of war. If there were no others, the importance of the war establishment in each society might in fact decline to the subordinate level it is believed to occupy. And the elimination of war would indeed be the procedural matter that the disarmament scenarios suggest.

But there are other, broader, more profoundly felt functions of war in modern societies. It is these invisible, or implied, functions that maintain war-readiness as the dominant force in our societies. And it is the unwillingness or inability of the writers of disarmament scenarios and reconversion plans to take them into account that has so reduced the usefulness of their work, and that has made it seem unrelated to the world we know.

THE FUNCTIONS OF WAR

A S WE HAVE INDICATED, the preeminence of the concept of war as the principal organizing force in most societies has been insufficiently appreciated. This is also true of its extensive effects throughout the many nonmilitary activities of society. These effects are less apparent in complex industrial societies like our own than in primitive cultures, the activities of which can be more easily and fully comprehended.

We propose in this section to examine these nonmilitary, implied, and usually invisible functions of war, to the extent that they bear on the problems of transition to peace for our society. The military, or ostensible, function of the war system requires no elaboration; it serves simply to defend or advance the "national interest" by means of organized violence. It is often necessary for a national military establishment to create a need for its unique powers—to maintain the franchise, so to speak. And a healthy military apparatus requires regular "exercise," by whatever rationale seems expedient, to prevent its atrophy.

The nonmilitary functions of the war system are more basic. They exist not merely to justify themselves but to serve broader social purposes. If and when war is eliminated, the military functions it has served will end with it. But its nonmilitary functions will not. It is essential, therefore, that we understand their significance before we can reasonably expect to evaluate whatever institutions may be proposed to replace them.

Economic

The production of weapons of mass destruction has always been associated with economic "waste." The term is pejorative, since it implies a failure of function. But no human activity can properly be considered wasteful if it achieves its contextual objective. The phrase "wasteful but necessary," applied not only to war expenditures but to most of the "unproductive" commercial activities of our society, is a contradiction in terms. ". . . The attacks that have since the time of Samuel's criticism of King Saul been leveled against military expenditures as waste may well have concealed or misunderstood the point that some kinds of waste may have a larger social utility."[1]

In the case of military "waste," there is indeed a larger social utility. It derives from the fact that the "wastefulness" of war production is exercised entirely outside the framework of the economy of supply and demand. As such, it provides the only critically large segment of the total economy that is subject to complete and arbitrary central control. If modern industrial societies can be defined as those which have developed the capacity to produce more than is required for their economic survival (regardless of the equities of distribution of goods within them), military spending can be said to furnish the only balance wheel with sufficient inertia to stabilize the advance of their economies. The fact that war is "wasteful" is what enables it to serve this function. And the faster the economy advances, the heavier this balance wheel must be.

This function is often viewed, oversimply, as a device

for the control of surpluses. One writer on the subject puts it this way: "Why is war so wonderful? Because it creates artificial demand . . . the only kind of artificial demand, moreover, that does not raise any political issues: *war, and only war, solves the problem of inventory.*"[2] The reference here is to shooting war, but it applies equally to the general war economy as well. "It is generally agreed," concludes, more cautiously, the report of a panel set up by the U.S. Arms Control and Disarmament Agency, "that the greatly expanded public sector since World War II, resulting from heavy defense expenditures, has provided additional protection against depressions, since this sector is not responsive to contraction in the private sector and has provided a sort of buffer or balance wheel in the economy."[3]

The *principal* economic function of war, in our view, is that it provides just such a flywheel. It is not to be confused in function with the various forms of fiscal control, none of which directly engages vast numbers of men and units of production. It is not to be confused with massive government expenditures in social welfare programs; once initiated, such programs normally become integral parts of the general economy and are no longer subject to arbitrary control.

But even in the context of the general civilian economy war cannot be considered wholly "wasteful." Without a long-established war economy, and without its frequent eruption into large-scale shooting war, most of the major industrial advances known to history, beginning with the development of iron, could never have taken place. Weapons technology structures the economy. According to the writer cited above, "Nothing is more ironic or revealing about our society than the fact that hugely destructive war is a very progressive force in it. . . . War production is progressive because it is production that would not otherwise have taken place. (It is not so widely appreciated, for example, that the civilian standard of living *rose* during World War II.)"[4] This is not "ironic or revealing," but essentially a simple statement of fact.

It should also be noted that war production has a dependably stimulating effect outside itself. Far from constituting a "wasteful" drain on the economy, war spending, considered pragmatically, has been a consistently positive factor in the rise of gross national product and of individual productivity. A former Secretary of the Army has carefully phrased it for public consumption thus: "If there is, as I suspect there is, a direct relation between the stimulus of large defense spending and a substantially increased rate of growth of gross national product, it quite simply follows that defense spending *per se* might be countenanced *on economic grounds alone* [emphasis added] as a stimulator of the national metabolism."[5] Actually, the fundamental nonmilitary utility of war in the economy is far more widely acknowledged than the scarcity of such affirmations as that quoted above would suggest.

But *negatively* phrased public recognitions of the importance of war to the general economy abound. The most familiar example is the effect of "peace threats" on the stock market, e.g., "Wall Street was shaken yesterday by news of an apparent peace feeler from North Vietnam, but swiftly recovered its composure after about an hour of sometimes indiscriminate selling."[6] Savings banks solicit deposits with similar cautionary slogans, e.g., "If peace breaks out, will you be ready for it?" A more subtle case in point was the recent refusal of the Department of Defense to permit the West German government to substitute nonmilitary goods for unwanted armaments in its purchase commitments from the United States; the decisive consideration was that the German purchases should not affect the general (nonmilitary) economy. Other incidental examples are to be found in the pressures brought to bear on the Department when it announces plans to close down an obsolete facility (as a "wasteful" form of "waste"), and in the usual coordination of stepped-up military activities (as in Vietnam in 1965) with dangerously rising unemployment rates.

Although we do not imply that a substitute for war in the economy cannot be devised, no combination of techniques for controlling employment, production, and consumption has yet been tested that can remotely compare to it in effectiveness. It is, and has been, the essential economic stabilizer of modern societies.

Political

The political functions of war have been up to now even more critical to social stability. It is not surprising, nevertheless, that discussions of economic conversion for peace tend to fall silent on the matter of political implementation, and that disarmament scenarios, often sophisticated in their weighing of international political factors, tend to disregard the political functions of the war system within individual societies.

These functions are essentially organizational. First of all, the existence of a society as a political "nation" requires as part of its definition an attitude of relationship toward other "nations." This is what we usually call a foreign policy. But a nation's foreign policy can have no substance if it lacks the means of enforcing its attitude toward other nations. It can do this in a credible manner only if it implies the threat of maximum political organization for this purpose—which is to say that it is organized to some degree for war. War, then, as we have defined it to include all national activities that recognize the possibility of armed conflict, is itself the defining element of any nation's existence vis-à-vis any other nation. Since it is historically axiomatic that the existence of any form of weaponry insures its use, we have used the word "peace" as virtually synonymous with disarmament. By the same token, "war" is virtually synonymous with nationhood. The elimination of war implies the inevitable elimination of national sovereignty and the traditional nation-state.

The war system not only has been essential to the existence of nations as independent political entities, but has been equally indispensable to their stable internal political structure. Without it, no government has ever been able to obtain acquiescence in its "legitimacy," or right to rule its society. The possibility of war provides the sense of external necessity without which no government can long remain in power. The historical record reveals one instance after another where the failure of a regime to maintain the credibility of a war threat led to its dissolution, by the forces of private interest, of reactions to social injustice, or of other disintegrative elements. The organization of a society for the possibility of war is its principal political stabilizer. It is ironic that this primary function of war has been generally recognized by historians only where it has been expressly acknowledged—in the pirate societies of the great conquerors.

The basic authority of a modern state over its people resides in its war powers. (There is, in fact, good reason to believe that codified law had its origins in the rules of conduct established by military victors for dealing with the defeated enemy, which were later adapted to apply to all

subject populations.[7]) On a day-to-day basis, it is represented by the institution of police, armed organizations
charged expressly with dealing with "internal enemies" in
a military manner. Like the conventional "external" military, the police are also substantially exempt from many
civilian legal restraints on their social behavior. In some
countries, the artificial distinction between police and
other military forces does not exist. On the long-term
basis, a government's emergency war powers—inherent in
the structure of even the most libertarian of nations—
define the most significant aspect of the relation between
state and citizen.

In advanced modern democratic societies, the war system has provided political leaders with another political-
economic function of increasing importance: it has served
as the last great safeguard against the elimination of necessary social classes. As economic productivity increases to a
level further and further above that of minimum subsis-
tence, it becomes more and more difficult for a society to
maintain distribution patterns insuring the existence of
"hewers of wood and drawers of water." The further
progress of automation can be expected to differentiate
still more sharply between "superior" workers and what
Ricardo called "menials," while simultaneously aggravat-
ing the problem of maintaining an unskilled labor supply.

The arbitrary nature of war expenditures and of other
military activities makes them ideally suited to control
these essential class relationships. Obviously, if the war
system were to be discarded, new political machinery
would be needed at once to serve this vital subfunction.
Until it is developed, the continuance of the war system
must be assured, if for no other reason, among others, than
to preserve whatever quality and degree of poverty a soci-

ety requires as an incentive, as well as to maintain the stability of its internal organization of power.

Sociological

Under this heading, we will examine a nexus of functions served by the war system that affect human behavior in society. In general, they are broader in application and less susceptible to direct observation than the economic and political factors previously considered.

The most obvious of these functions is the time-honored use of military institutions to provide antisocial elements with an acceptable role in the social structure. The disintegrative, unstable social movements loosely described as "fascist" have traditionally taken root in societies that have lacked adequate military or paramilitary outlets to meet the needs of these elements. This function has been critical in periods of rapid change. The danger signals are easy to recognize, even though the stigmata bear different names at different times. The current euphemistic clichés—"juvenile delinquency" and "alienation"—have had their counterparts in every age. In earlier days these conditions were dealt with directly by the military without the complications of due process, usually through press gangs or outright enslavement. But it is not hard to visualize, for example, the degree of social disruption that might have taken place in the United States during the last two decades if the problem of the socially disaffected of the post-World War II period had not been foreseen and effectively met. The younger, and more dangerous, of these hostile social groupings have been kept under control by the Selective Service System.

This system and its analogues elsewhere furnish remarkably clear examples of disguised military utility.

Informed persons in this country have never accepted the official rationale for a peacetime draft—military necessity, preparedness, etc.—as worthy of serious consideration. But what has gained credence among thoughtful men is the rarely voiced, less easily refuted, proposition that the institution of military service has a "patriotic" priority in our society that must be maintained for its own sake. Ironically, the simplistic official justification for selective service comes closer to the mark, once the nonmilitary functions of military institutions are understood. As a control device over the hostile, nihilistic, and potentially unsettling elements of a society in transition, the draft can again be defended, and quite convincingly, as a "military" necessity.

Nor can it be considered a coincidence that overt military activity, and thus the level of draft calls, tend to follow the major fluctuations in the unemployment rate in the lower age groups. This rate, in turn, is a time-tested herald of social discontent. It must be noted also that the armed forces in every civilization have provided the principal state-supported haven for what we now call the "unemployable." The typical European standing army (of fifty years ago) consisted of ". . . troops unfit for employment in commerce, industry, or agriculture, led by officers unfit to practice any legitimate profession or to conduct a business enterprise."[8] This is still largely true, if less apparent. In a sense, this function of the military as the custodian of the economically or culturally deprived was the forerunner of most contemporary civilian social-welfare programs, from the W.P.A. to various forms of "socialized" medicine and social security. It is interesting that liberal sociologists currently proposing to use the Selective Service System as a medium of cultural upgrading of the poor consider this a *novel* application of military practice.

Although it cannot be said absolutely that such critical measures of social control as the draft require a military rationale, no modern society has yet been willing to risk experimentation with any other kind. Even during such periods of comparatively simple social crisis as the so-called Great Depression of the 1930s, it was deemed prudent by the government to invest minor make-work projects, like the "Civilian" Conservation Corps, with a military character, and to place the more ambitious National Recovery Administration under the direction of a professional army officer at its inception. Today, at least one small Northern European country, plagued with uncontrollable unrest among its "alienated youth," is considering the expansion of its armed forces, despite the problem of making credible the expansion of a nonexistent external threat.

Sporadic efforts have been made to promote general recognition of broad national values free of military connotation, but they have been ineffective. For example, to enlist public support of even such modest programs of social adjustment as "fighting inflation" or "maintaining physical fitness" it has been necessary for the government to utilize a patriotic (i.e., military) incentive. It sells "defense" bonds and it equates health with military preparedness. This is not surprising; since the concept of "nationhood" implies readiness for war, a "national" program must do likewise.

In general, the war system provides the basic motivation for primary social organization. In so doing, it reflects on the societal level the incentives of individual human behavior. The most important of these, for social purposes, is the individual psychological rationale for allegiance to a society and its values. Allegiance requires a cause; a cause requires an enemy. This much is obvious; the critical point is that the enemy that defines the cause must seem genuinely formidable. Roughly speaking, the presumed power of the "enemy" sufficient to warrant an individual sense of allegiance to a society must be proportionate to the size and complexity of the society. Today, of course, that power must be one of unprecedented magnitude and frightfulness.

It follows, from the patterns of human behavior, that the credibility of a social "enemy" demands similarly a readiness of response in proportion to its menace. In a broad social context, "an eye for an eye" still characterizes the only acceptable attitude toward a presumed threat of aggression, despite contrary religious and moral precepts governing personal conduct. The remoteness of personal decision from social consequence in a modern society makes it easy for its members to maintain this attitude without being aware of it. A recent example is the war in Vietnam; a less recent one was the bombing of Hiroshima and Nagasaki.[9] In each case, the extent and gratuitousness of the slaughter were abstracted into political formulae by most Americans, once the proposition that the victims were "enemies" was established. The war system makes such an abstracted response possible in nonmilitary contexts as well. A conventional example of this mechanism is the inability of most people to connect, let us say, the starvation of millions in India with their own past conscious political decision-making. Yet the sequential logic linking a decision to restrict grain production in America with an eventual famine in Asia is obvious, unambiguous, and unconcealed.

What gives the war system its preeminent role in social

organization, as elsewhere, is its unmatched authority over life and death. It must be emphasized again that the war system is not a mere social extension of the presumed need for individual human violence, but itself in turn serves to rationalize most nonmilitary killing. It also provides the precedent for the collective willingness of members of a society to pay a blood price for institutions far less central to social organization than war. To take a handy example, ". . . rather than accept speed limits of twenty miles an hour we prefer to let automobiles kill forty thousand people a year."[10] A Rand analyst puts it in more general terms and less rhetorically: "I am sure that there is, in effect, a desirable level of automobile accidents—desirable, that is, from a broad point of view; in the sense that it is a necessary concomitant of things of greater value to society."[11] The point may seem too obvious for iteration, but it is essential to an understanding of the important motivational function of war as a model for collective sacrifice.

A brief look at some defunct premodern societies is instructive. One of the most noteworthy features common to the larger, more complex, and more successful of ancient civilizations was their widespread use of the blood sacrifice. If one were to limit consideration to those cultures whose regional hegemony was so complete that the prospect of "war" had become virtually inconceivable—as was the case with several of the great pre-Columbian societies of the Western Hemisphere—it would be found that some form of ritual killing occupied a position of paramount social importance in each. Invariably, the ritual was invested with mythic or religious significance; as with all religious and totemic practice, however, the ritual masked a broader and more important social function.

In these societies, the blood sacrifice served the purpose of maintaining a vestigial "earnest" of the society's capability and willingness to make war—i.e., kill and be killed—in the event that some mystical—i.e., unforeseen—circumstance were to give rise to the possibility. That the "earnest" was not an adequate substitute for genuine military organization when the unthinkable enemy, such as the Spanish conquistadores, actually appeared on the scene in no way negates the function of the ritual. It was primarily, if not exclusively, a symbolic reminder that war had once been the central organizing force of the society, and that this condition might recur.

It does not follow that a transition to total peace in modern societies would require the use of this model, even in less "barbaric" guise. But the historical analogy serves as a reminder that a viable substitute for war as a social system cannot be a mere symbolic charade. It must involve real risk of real personal destruction, and on a scale consistent with the size and complexity of modern social systems. Credibility is the key. Whether the substitute is ritual in nature or functionally substantive, unless it provides a believable life-and-death threat it will not serve the socially organizing function of war.

The existence of an accepted external menace, then, is essential to social cohesiveness as well as to the acceptance of political authority. The menace must be believable, it must be of a magnitude consistent with the complexity of the society threatened, and it must appear, at least, to affect the entire society.

Ecological

Man, like all other animals, is subject to the continuing process of adapting to the limitations of his environment.

But the principal mechanism he has utilized for this purpose is unique among living creatures. To forestall the inevitable historical cycles of inadequate food supply, post-Neolithic man destroys surplus members of his own species by organized warfare.

Ethologists[12] have often observed that the organized slaughter of members of their own species is virtually unknown among other animals. Man's special propensity to kill his own kind (shared to a limited degree with rats) may be attributed to his inability to adapt anachronistic patterns of survival (like primitive hunting) to his development of "civilizations" in which these patterns cannot be effectively sublimated. It may be attributed to other causes that have been suggested, such as a maladapted "territorial instinct," etc. Nevertheless, it exists and its social expression in war constitutes a biological control of his relationship to his natural environment that is peculiar to man alone.

War has served to help assure the *survival* of the human species. But as an evolutionary device to *improve* it, war is almost unbelievably inefficient. With few exceptions, the selective processes of other living creatures promote both specific survival *and* genetic improvement. When a conventionally adaptive animal faces one of its periodic crises of insufficiency, it is the "inferior" members of the species that normally disappear. An animal's social response to such a crisis may take the form of a mass migration, during which the weak fall by the wayside. Or it may follow the dramatic and more efficient pattern of lemming societies, in which the weaker members voluntarily disperse, leaving available food supplies for the stronger. In either case, the strong survive and the weak fall. In human societies, those who fight and die in wars for survival are in general its biologically stronger members. This is natural selection in reverse.

The regressive genetic effect of war has been often noted[13] and equally often deplored, even when it confuses biological and cultural factors.[14] The disproportionate loss of the *biologically* stronger remains inherent in traditional warfare. It serves to underscore the fact that survival of the species, rather than its improvement, is the fundamental purpose of natural selection, if it can be said to have a purpose, just as it is the basic premise of this study.

But as the polemologist Gaston Bouthoul[15] has pointed out, other institutions that were developed to serve this ecological function have proved even less satisfactory. (They include such established forms as these: infanticide, practiced chiefly in ancient and primitive societies; sexual mutilation; monasticism; forced emigration; extensive capital punishment, as in old China and eighteenth-century England; and other similar, usually localized, practices.)

Man's ability to increase his productivity of the essentials of physical life suggests that the need for protection against cyclical famine may be nearly obsolete.[16] It has thus tended to reduce the apparent importance of the basic ecological function of war, which is generally disregarded by peace theorists. Two aspects of it remain especially relevant, however. The first is obvious: current rates of population growth, compounded by environmental threat of chemical and other contaminants, may well bring about a new crisis of insufficiency. If so, it is likely to be one of unprecedented global magnitude, not merely regional or temporary. Conventional methods of warfare would almost surely prove inadequate, in this event, to reduce the consuming population to a level consistent with survival of the species.

The second relevant factor is the efficiency of modern methods of mass destruction. Even if their use is not required to meet a world population crisis, they offer, perhaps paradoxically, the first opportunity in the history of man to halt the regressive genetic effects of natural selection by war. Nuclear weapons are indiscriminate. Their application would bring to an end the disproportionate destruction of the physically stronger members of the species (the "warriors") in periods of war. Whether this prospect of genetic gain would offset the unfavorable mutations anticipated from postnuclear radioactivity we have not yet determined. What gives the question a bearing on our study is the possibility that the determination may yet have to be made.

Another secondary ecological trend bearing on projected population growth is the regressive effect of certain medical advances. Pestilence, for example, is no longer an important factor in population control. The problem of increased life expectancy has been aggravated. These advances also pose a potentially more sinister problem, in that undesirable genetic traits that were formerly self-liquidating are now medically maintained. Many diseases that were once fatal at preprocreational ages are now cured; the effect of this development is to perpetuate undesirable susceptibilities and mutations. It seems clear that a new quasi-eugenic function of war is now in process of formation that will have to be taken into account in any transition plan. For the time being, the Department of Defense appears to have recognized such factors, as has been demonstrated by the planning under way by the Rand Corporation to cope with the breakdown in the ecological balance anticipated after a thermonuclear war. The Department has also begun to stockpile birds, for example, against the expected proliferation of radiation-resistant insects, etc.

Cultural and Scientific

The declared order of values in modern societies gives a high place to the so-called "creative" activities, and an even higher one to those associated with the advance of scientific knowledge. Widely held social values can be translated into political equivalents, which in turn may bear on the nature of a transition to peace. The attitudes of those who hold these values must be taken into account in the planning of the transition. The dependence, therefore, of cultural and scientific achievement on the war system would be an important consideration in a transition plan even if such achievement had no inherently necessary social function.

Of all the countless dichotomies invented by scholars to account for the major differences in art styles and cycles, only one has been consistently unambiguous in its application to a variety of forms and cultures. However it may be verbalized, the basic distinction is this: Is the work war-oriented or is it not? Among primitive peoples, the war dance is the most important art form. Elsewhere, literature, music, painting, sculpture, and architecture that has won lasting acceptance has invariably dealt with a theme of war, expressly or implicitly, and has expressed the centricity of war to society. The war in question may be national conflict, as in Shakespeare plays, Beethoven's music, or Goya's paintings, or it may be reflected in the form of religious, social, or moral struggle, as in the work of Dante, Rembrandt, and Bach. Art that cannot be classi-

fied as war-oriented is usually described as "sterile,"
"decadent," and so on. Application of the "war standard"
to works of art may often leave room for debate in individual cases, but there is no question of its role as the fundamental determinant of cultural values. Aesthetic and
moral standards have a common anthropological origin, in
the exaltation of bravery, the willingness to kill and risk
death in tribal warfare.

It is also instructive to note that the character of a society's culture has borne a close relationship to its war-making potential, in the context of its times. It is no accident
that the current "cultural explosion" in the United States is
taking place during an era marked by an unusually rapid
advance in weaponry. This relationship is more generally
recognized than the literature on the subject would suggest. For example, many artists and writers are now beginning to express concern over the limited creative options
they envisage in the warless world they think, or hope,
may be soon upon us. They are currently preparing for
this possibility by unprecedented experimentation with
meaningless forms; their interest in recent years has been
increasingly engaged by the abstract pattern, the gratu-
itous emotion, the random happening, and the unrelated
sequence.

The relationship of war to scientific research and dis-
covery is more explicit. War is the principal motivational
force for the development of science at every level, from
the abstractly conceptual to the narrowly technological.
Modern society places a high value on "pure" science, but
it is historically inescapable that all the significant discoveries that have been made about the natural world have
been inspired by the real or imaginary military necessities
of their epochs. The consequences of the discoveries have

indeed gone far afield, but war has always provided the basic incentive.

Beginning with the development of iron and steel, and proceeding through the discoveries of the laws of motion and thermodynamics to the age of the atomic particle, the synthetic polymer, and the space capsule, no important scientific advance has not been at least indirectly initiated by an implicit requirement of weaponry. More prosaic examples include the transistor radio (an outgrowth of military communications requirements), the assembly line (from Civil War firearms needs), the steel-frame building (from the steel battleship), the canal lock, and so on. A typical adaptation can be seen in a device as modest as the common lawnmower; it developed from the revolving scythe devised by Leonardo da Vinci to precede a horse-powered vehicle into enemy ranks.

The most direct relationship can be found in medical technology. For example, a giant "walking machine," an amplifier of body motions invented for military use in difficult terrain, is now making it possible for many previously confined to wheelchairs to walk. The Vietnam war alone has led to spectacular improvements in amputation procedures, blood-handling techniques, and surgical logistics. It has stimulated new large-scale research on malaria and other tropical parasite diseases; it is hard to estimate how long this work would otherwise have been delayed, despite its enormous nonmilitary importance to nearly half the world's population.

Other

We have elected to omit from our discussion of the nonmilitary functions of war those we do not consider critical to a transition program. This is not to say they are unimportant, however, but only that they appear to present no special problems for the organization of a peace-oriented social system. They include the following:

War as a general social release. This is a psychosocial function, serving the same purpose for a society as do the holiday, the celebration, and the orgy for the individual— the release and redistribution of undifferentiated tensions. War provides for the periodic necessary readjustment of standards of social behavior (the "moral climate") and for the dissipation of general boredom, one of the most consistently undervalued and unrecognized of social phenomena.

War as a generational stabilizer. This psychological function, served by other behavior patterns in other animals, enables the physically deteriorating older generation to maintain its control of the younger, destroying it if necessary.

War as an ideological clarifier. The dualism that characterizes the traditional dialectic of all branches of philosophy and of stable political relationships stems from war as the prototype of conflict. Except for secondary considerations, there cannot be, to put it as simply as possible, more than two sides to a question because there cannot be more than two sides to a war.

War as the basis for inter-national understanding. Before the development of modern communications, the strategic requirements of war provided the only substantial incentive for the enrichment of one national culture with the achievements of another. Although this is still the case in many inter-national relationships, the function is obsolescent.

We have also forgone extended characterization of those functions we assume to be widely and explicitly recognized. An obvious example is the role of war as controller of the quality and degree of unemployment. This is more than an economic and political subfunction; its sociological, cultural, and ecological aspects are also important, although often teleonomic. But none affect the general problem of substitution. The same is true of certain other functions; those we have included are sufficient to define the scope of the problem.

SUBSTITUTES FOR
THE FUNCTIONS OF WAR

B Y NOW IT SHOULD BE CLEAR that the most detailed and comprehensive master plan for a transition to world peace will remain academic if it fails to deal forthrightly with the problem of the critical nonmilitary functions of war. The social needs they serve are essential; if the war system no longer exists to meet them, substitute institutions will have to be established for the purpose. These surrogates must be "realistic," which is to say of a scope and nature that can be conceived and implemented in the context of present-day social capabilities. This is not the truism it may appear to be; the requirements of radical social change often reveal the distinction between a most conservative projection and a wildly utopian scheme to be fine indeed.

In this section we will consider some possible substitutes for these functions. Only in rare instances have they been put forth for the purposes which concern us here, but we see no reason to limit ourselves to proposals that address themselves explicitly to the problem as we have outlined it. We will disregard the ostensible, or military, functions of war; it is a premise of this study that the transition to peace implies absolutely that they will no longer exist in any relevant sense. We will also disregard the noncritical functions exemplified at the end of the preceding section.

Economic

Economic surrogates for war must meet two principal criteria. They must be "wasteful," in the common sense of the word, and they must operate outside the normal supply-demand system. A corollary that should be obvious is that the magnitude of the waste must be sufficient to meet the needs of a particular society. An economy as advanced and complex as our own requires the planned average annual destruction of not less than 10 percent of gross national product[1] if it is effectively to fulfill its stabilizing function. When the mass of a balance wheel is inadequate to the power it is intended to control, its effect can be self-defeating, as with a runaway locomotive. The analogy, though crude,[2] is especially apt for the American economy, as our record of cyclical depressions shows. All have taken place during periods of grossly inadequate military spending.

Those few economic conversion programs which by implication acknowledge the nonmilitary economic function of war (at least to some extent) tend to assume that so-called social-welfare expenditures will fill the vacuum created by the disappearance of military spending. When one considers the backlog of unfinished business—proposed but still unexecuted—in this field, the assumption seems plausible. Let us examine briefly the following list, which is more or less typical of general social-welfare programs.[3]

Health. Drastic expansion of medical research, education, and training facilities; hospital and clinic construction; the general objective of *complete* government-guaranteed health care for all, at a level consistent with current developments in medical technology.

Education. The equivalent of the foregoing in teacher training; schools and libraries; the drastic upgrading of standards, with the general objective of making available for all an attainable educational goal equivalent to what is now considered a professional degree.

Housing. Clean, comfortable, safe, and spacious living space for all, at the level now enjoyed by about 15 percent of the population in this country (less in most others).

Transportation. The establishment of a system of mass public transportation making it possible for all to travel to and from areas of work and recreation quickly, comfortably, and conveniently, and to travel privately for pleasure rather than necessity.

Physical environment. The development and protection of water supplies, forests, parks, and other natural resources; the elimination of chemical and bacterial contaminants from air, water, and soil.

Poverty. The genuine elimination of poverty, defined by a standard consistent with current economic productivity, by means of a guaranteed annual income or whatever system of distribution will best assure its achievement.

This is only a sampler of the more obvious domestic social welfare items, and we have listed it in a deliberately broad, perhaps extravagant, manner. In the past, such a vague and ambitious-sounding "program" would have been dismissed out of hand, without serious consideration; it would clearly have been, *prima facie*, far too costly, quite apart from its political implications.[4] Our objection to it, on the other hand, could hardly be more contradictory. As an economic substitute for war, it is inadequate because it would be far too cheap.

If this seems paradoxical, it must be remembered that up to now all proposed social-welfare expenditures have had to be measured *within* the war economy, not as a replacement for it. The old slogan about a battleship or an

ICBM costing as much as x hospitals or y schools or z homes takes on a very different meaning if there are to be no more battleships or ICBM's.

Since the list is general, we have elected to forestall the tangential controversy that surrounds arbitrary cost projections by offering no individual cost estimates. But the maximum program that could be physically effected along the lines indicated could approach the established level of military spending only for a limited time—in our opinion, subject to a detailed cost-and-feasibility analysis, less than ten years. In this short period, at this rate, the major goals of the program would have been achieved. Its capital-investment phase would have been completed, and it would have established a permanent comparatively modest level of annual operating cost—*within the framework of the general economy.*

Here is the basic weakness of the social-welfare surrogate. On the short-term basis, a maximum program of this sort could replace a normal military spending program, provided it was designed, like the military model, to be subject to arbitrary control. Public housing starts, for example, or the development of modern medical centers might be accelerated or halted from time to time, as the requirements of a stable economy might dictate. But on the long-term basis, social-welfare spending, no matter how often redefined, would necessarily become an integral, accepted part of the economy, of no more value as a stabilizer than the automobile industry or old age and survivors' insurance. Apart from whatever merit social-welfare programs are deemed to have for their own sake, their function as a substitute for war in the economy would thus be self-liquidating. They might serve, however, as expedients pending the development of more durable substitute measures.

Another economic surrogate that has been proposed is a series of giant "space-research" programs. These have already demonstrated their utility in more modest scale within the military economy. What has been implied, although not yet expressly put forth, is the development of a long-range sequence of space-research projects with largely unattainable goals. This kind of program offers several advantages lacking in the social-welfare model. First, it is unlikely to phase itself out, regardless of the predictable "surprises" science has in store for us: the universe is too big. In the event some individual project unexpectedly succeeds there would be no dearth of substitute problems. For example, if colonization of the moon proceeds on schedule, it could then become "necessary" to establish a beachhead on Mars or Jupiter, and so on. Second, it need be no more dependent on the general supply-demand economy than its military prototype. Third, it lends itself extraordinarily well to arbitrary control.

Space research can be viewed as the nearest modern equivalent yet devised to the pyramid-building, and similar ritualistic enterprises, of ancient societies. It is true that the scientific value of the space program, even of what has already been accomplished, is substantial on its own terms. But current programs are absurdly and obviously disproportionate, in the relationship of the knowledge sought to the expenditures committed. All but a small fraction of the space budget, measured by the standards of comparable scientific objectives, must be charged *de facto* to the military economy. Future space research, projected as a war surrogate, would further reduce the "scientific" rationale of its budget to a minuscule percentage indeed.

As a purely economic substitute for war, therefore, extension of the space program warrants serious consideration.

In Section 3 we pointed out that certain disarmament models, which we called conservative, postulated extremely expensive and elaborate inspection systems. Would it be possible to extend and institutionalize such systems to the point where they might serve as economic surrogates for war spending? The organization of fail-safe inspection machinery could well be ritualized in a manner similar to that of established military processes. "Inspection teams" might be very like armies, and their technical equipment might be very like weapons. Inflating the inspection budget to military scale presents no difficulty. The appeal of this kind of scheme lies in the comparative ease of transition between two parallel systems.

The "elaborate inspection" surrogate is fundamentally fallacious, however. Although it might be economically useful, as well as politically necessary, during the disarmament transition, it would fail as a substitute for the economic function of war for one simple reason. Peacekeeping inspection is part of a war system, not of a peace system. It implies the possibility of weapons maintenance or manufacture, which could not exist in a world at peace as here defined. Massive inspection also implies sanctions, and thus war-readiness.

The same fallacy is more obvious in plans to create a patently useless "defense conversion" apparatus. The long-discredited proposal to build "total" civil defense facilities is one example; another is the plan to establish a giant antimissile missile complex (Nike-X, *et al.*). These programs, of course, are economic rather than strategic. Nevertheless, they are not substitutes for military spending but merely different forms of it.

A more sophisticated variant is the proposal to estab-lish the "Unarmed Forces" of the United States.[5] This would conveniently maintain the entire institutional mili-tary structure, redirecting it essentially toward social-wel-fare activities on a global scale. It would be, in effect, a giant military Peace Corps. There is nothing inherently unworkable about this plan, and using the existing mili-tary system to effectuate its own demise is both ingenious and convenient. But even on a greatly magnified world basis, social-welfare expenditures must sooner or later reenter the atmosphere of the normal economy. The practi-cal transitional virtues of such a scheme would thus be eventually negated by its inadequacy as a permanent eco-nomic stabilizer.

Political

The war system makes the stable government of soci-eties possible. It does this essentially by providing an external necessity for a society to accept political rule. In so doing, it establishes the basis for nationhood and the authority of government to control its constituents. What other institution or combination of programs might serve these functions in its place?

We have already pointed out that the end of war means the end of national sovereignty, and thus the end of nation-hood as we know it today. But this does not necessarily mean the end of nations in the administrative sense, and internal political power will remain essential to a stable society. The emerging "nations" of the peace epoch must continue to draw political authority from some source.

A number of proposals have been made governing the relations between nations after total disarmament; all are basically juridical in nature. They contemplate institutions more or less like a World Court, or a United Nations, but vested with real authority. They may or may not serve their ostensible postmilitary purpose of settling international disputes, but we need not discuss that here. None would offer effective external pressure on a peace-world nation to organize itself politically.

It might be argued that a well-armed international police force, operating under the authority of such a supranational "court," could well serve the function of external enemy. This, however, would constitute a military operation, like the inspection schemes mentioned, and, like them, would be inconsistent with the premise of an end to the war system. It is possible that a variant of the "Unarmed Forces" idea might be developed in such a way that its "constructive" (i.e., social-welfare) activities could be combined with an economic "threat" of sufficient size and credibility to warrant political organization. Would this kind of threat also be contradictory to our basic premise?—that is, would it be inevitably military? Not necessarily, in our view, but we are skeptical of its capacity to evoke credibility. Also, the obvious destabilizing effect of any global social-welfare surrogate on politically necessary class relationships would create an entirely new set of transition problems at least equal in magnitude.

Credibility, in fact, lies at the heart of the problem of developing a political substitute for war. This is where the space-race proposals, in many ways so well suited as economic substitutes for war, fall short. The most ambitious and unrealistic space project cannot of itself generate a believable external menace. It has been hotly argued[6] that such a menace would offer the "last, best hope of peace," etc., by uniting mankind against the danger of destruction by "creatures" from other planets or from outer space. Experiments have been proposed to test the credibility of an out-of-our-world invasion threat; it is possible that a few of the more difficult-to-explain "flying saucer" incidents of recent years were in fact early experiments of this kind. If so, they could hardly have been judged encouraging. We anticipate no difficulties in making a "need" for a giant super space program credible for economic purposes, even were there not ample precedent; extending it, for political purposes, to include features unfortunately associated with science fiction would obviously be a more dubious undertaking.

Nevertheless, an effective political substitute for war would require "alternate enemies," some of which might seem equally farfetched in the context of the current war system. It may be, for instance, that gross pollution of the environment can eventually replace the possibility of mass destruction by nuclear weapons as the principal apparent threat to the survival of the species. Poisoning of the air, and of the principal sources of food and water supply, is already well advanced, and at first glance would seem promising in this respect; it constitutes a threat that can be dealt with only through social organization and political power. But from present indications it will be a generation to a generation and a half before environmental pollution, however severe, will be sufficiently menacing, on a global scale, to offer a possible basis for a solution.

It is true that the rate of pollution could be increased selectively for this purpose; in fact, the mere modifying of existing programs for the deterrence of pollution could speed up the process enough to make the threat credible much sooner. But the pollution problem has been so widely publicized in recent years that it seems highly improbable that a program of deliberate environmental poisoning could be implemented in a politically acceptable manner.

However unlikely some of the possible alternate enemies we have mentioned may seem, we must emphasize that one *must* be found, of credible quality and magnitude, if a transition to peace is ever to come about without social disintegration. It is more probable, in our judgment, that such a threat will have to be invented, rather than developed from unknown conditions. For this reason, we believe further speculation about its putative nature ill-advised in this context. Since there is considerable doubt, in our minds, that *any* viable political surrogate can be devised, we are reluctant to compromise, by premature discussion, any possible option that may eventually lie open to our government.

Sociological

Of the many functions of war we have found convenient to group together in this classification, two are critical. In a world of peace, the continuing stability of society will require: 1) an effective substitute for military institutions that can neutralize destabilizing social elements and 2) a credible motivational surrogate for war that can insure social cohesiveness. The first is an essential element of social control; the second is the basic mechanism for adapting individual human drives to the needs of society.

Most proposals that address themselves, explicitly or otherwise, to the postwar problem of controlling the socially alienated turn to some variant of the Peace Corps or the so-called Job Corps for a solution. The socially disaffected, the economically unprepared, the psychologically unconformable, the hard-core "delinquents," the incorrigible "subversives," and the rest of the unemployable are seen as somehow transformed by the disciplines of a service modeled on military precedent into more or less dedicated social service workers. This presumption also informs the otherwise hardheaded ratiocination of the "Unarmed Forces" plan.

The problem has been addressed, in the language of popular sociology, by Secretary McNamara. "Even in our abundant societies, we have reason enough to worry over the tensions that coil and tighten among underprivileged young people, and finally flail out in delinquency and crime. What are we to expect . . . where mounting frustrations are likely to fester into eruptions of violence and extremism?" In a seemingly unrelated passage, he continues: "It seems to me that we could move toward remedying that inequity [of the Selective Service System] by asking every young person in the United States to give two years of service to his country—whether in one of the military services, in the Peace Corps, or in some other volunteer developmental work at home or abroad. We could encourage other countries to do the same."[7] Here, as elsewhere throughout this significant speech, Mr. McNamara has focused, indirectly but unmistakably, on one of the key issues bearing on a possible transition to peace, and has later indicated, also indirectly, a rough approach to its resolution, again phrased in the language of the current war system.

It seems clear that Mr. McNamara and other proponents of the peace-corps surrogate for this war function lean heavily on the success of the paramilitary Depression programs mentioned in the last section. We find the precedent wholly inadequate in degree. Neither the lack of relevant precedent, however, nor the dubious social-welfare sentimentality characterizing this approach warrant its rejection without careful study. It may be viable—provided, first, that the military origin of the Corps format be effectively rendered out of its operational activity, and second, that the transition from paramilitary activities to "developmental work" can be effected without regard to the attitudes of the Corps personnel or to the "value" of the work it is expected to perform.

Another possible surrogate for the control of potential enemies of society is the reintroduction, in some form consistent with modern technology and political processes, of slavery. Up to now, this has been suggested only in fiction, notably in the works of Wells, Huxley, Orwell, and others engaged in the imaginative anticipation of the sociology of the future. But the fantasies projected in *Brave New World* and *1984* have seemed less and less implausible over the years since their publication. The traditional association of slavery with ancient preindustrial cultures should not blind us to its adaptability to advanced forms of social organization, nor should its equally traditional incompatibility with Western moral and economic values. It is entirely possible that the development of a sophisticated form of slavery may be an absolute prerequisite for social control in a world at peace. As a practical matter, conversion of the code of military discipline to a euphemized form of enslavement would entail surprisingly little revision; the logical first step would be the adoption of some form of "universal" military service.

When it comes to postulating a credible substitute for war capable of directing human behavior patterns in behalf of social organization, few options suggest themselves. Like its political function, the motivational function of war requires the existence of a genuinely menacing social enemy. The principal difference is that for purposes of motivating basic allegiance, as distinct from accepting political authority, the "alternate enemy" must imply a more immediate, tangible, and directly felt threat of destruction. It must justify the need for taking and paying a "blood price" in wide areas of human concern.

In this respect, the possible substitute enemies noted earlier would be insufficient. One exception might be the environmental-pollution model, if the danger to society it posed was genuinely imminent. The fictive models would have to carry the weight of extraordinary conviction, underscored with a not inconsiderable actual sacrifice of life; the construction of an up-to-date mythological or religious structure for this purpose would present difficulties in our era, but must certainly be considered.

Games theorists have suggested, in other contexts, the development of "blood games" for the effective control of individual aggressive impulses. It is an ironic commentary on the current state of war and peace studies that it was left not to scientists but to the makers of a commercial film[8] to develop a model for this notion, on the implausible level of popular melodrama, as a ritualized manhunt. More realistically, such a ritual might be socialized, in the manner of the Spanish Inquisition and the less formal witch trials of other periods, for purposes of "social purification," "state security," or other rationale both acceptable and credible to postwar societies. The feasibility of such an updated version of still another ancient institution, though doubtful, is considerably less fanciful than the wishful notion of many peace planners that a lasting condition of peace can be brought about without the most painstaking examination of every possible surrogate for the essential functions of war. What is involved here, in a sense, is the quest for William James's "moral equivalent of war."

It is also possible that the two functions considered under this heading may be jointly served, in the sense of establishing the antisocial, for whom a control institution is needed, as the "alternate enemy" needed to hold society together. The relentless and irreversible advance of unemployability at all levels of society, and the similar extension of generalized alienation from accepted values[9] may make some such program necessary even as an adjunct to the war system. As before, we will not speculate on the specific forms this kind of program might take, except to note that there is again ample precedent, in the treatment meted out to disfavored, allegedly menacing, ethnic groups in certain societies during certain historical periods.[10]

Ecological

Considering the shortcomings of war as a mechanism of selective population control, it might appear that devising substitutes for this function should be comparatively simple. Schematically this is so, but the problem of timing the transition to a new ecological balancing device makes the feasibility of substitution less certain.

It must be remembered that the limitation of war in this function is entirely eugenic. War has not been genetically progressive. But as a system of gross population control to preserve the species it cannot fairly be faulted. And, as has been pointed out, the nature of war is itself in transition. Current trends in warfare—the increased strategic bombing of civilians and the greater military importance now attached to the destruction of sources of supply (as opposed to purely "military" bases and personnel)—strongly suggest that a truly qualitative improvement is in the making. Assuming the war system is to continue, it is more than probable that the regressively selective quality of war will have been reversed, as its victims become more genetically representative of their societies.

There is no question but that a universal requirement that procreation be limited to the products of artificial insemination would provide a fully adequate substitute control for population levels. Such a reproductive system would, of course, have the added advantage of being susceptible of direct eugenic management. Its predictable further development—conception and embryonic growth taking place wholly under laboratory conditions—would extend these controls to their logical conclusion. The ecological function of war under these circumstances would not only be superseded but surpassed in effectiveness.

The indicated intermediate step—total control of conception with a variant of the ubiquitous "pill," via water supplies or certain essential foodstuffs, offset by a controlled "antidote"—is already under development.[11] There would appear to be no foreseeable need to revert to any of the outmoded practices referred to in the previous section (infanticide, etc.) as there might have been if the possibility of transition to peace had arisen two generations ago.

The real question here, therefore, does not concern the viability of this war substitute, but the political problems involved in bringing it about. It cannot be established while the war system is still in effect. The reason for this is simple: excess population is war material. As long as any society must contemplate even a remote possibility of war, it must maintain a maximum supportable population, even when so doing critically aggravates an economic liability. This is paradoxical, in view of war's role in reducing excess population, but it is readily understood. War controls the *general* population level, but the ecological interest of any single society lies in maintaining its hegemony vis-à-vis other societies. The obvious analogy can be seen in any free-enterprise economy. Practices damaging to the society as a whole—both competitive and monopolistic—are abetted by the conflicting economic motives of individual capital interests. The obvious precedent can be found in the seemingly irrational political difficulties which have blocked universal adoption of simple birth-control methods. Nations desperately in need of increasing unfavorable production-consumption ratios are nevertheless unwilling to gamble their possible military requirements of twenty years hence for this purpose. Unilateral population control, as practiced in ancient Japan and in other isolated societies, is out of the question in today's world.

Since the eugenic solution cannot be achieved until the transition to the peace system takes place, why not wait? One must qualify the inclination to agree. As we noted earlier, a real possibility of an unprecedented global crisis of insufficiency exists today, which the war system may not be able to forestall. If this should come to pass before an agreed-upon transition to peace were completed, the result might be irrevocably disastrous. There is clearly no solution to this dilemma; it is a risk which must be taken. But it tends to support the view that if a decision is made to eliminate the war system, it were better done sooner than later.

Cultural and Scientific

Strictly speaking, the function of war as the determinant of cultural values and as the prime mover of scientific progress may not be critical in a world without war. Our criterion for the basic nonmilitary functions of war has been: Are they necessary to the survival and stability of society? The absolute need for substitute cultural value-determinants and for the continued advance of scientific knowledge is not established. We believe it important, however, in behalf of those for whom these functions hold subjective significance, that it be known what they can reasonably expect in culture and science after a transition to peace.

So far as the creative arts are concerned, there is no reason to believe they would disappear, but only that they would change in character and relative social importance. The elimination of war would in due course deprive them of their principal conative force, but it would necessarily take some time for the effect of this withdrawal to be felt. During the transition, and perhaps for a generation thereafter, themes of sociomoral conflict inspired by the war system would be increasingly transferred to the idiom of purely personal sensibility. At the same time, a new aesthetic would have to develop. Whatever its name, form, or rationale, its function would be to express, in language appropriate to the new period, the once discredited philosophy that art exists for its own sake. This aesthetic would reject unequivocally the classic requirement of paramilitary conflict as the substantive content of great art. The eventual effect of the peace-world philosophy of art would be democratizing in the extreme, in the sense that a generally acknowledged subjectivity of artistic standards would equalize their new, content-free "values."

What may be expected to happen is that art would be reassigned the role it once played in a few primitive peace-oriented social systems. This was the function of pure decoration, entertainment, or play, entirely free of the burden of expressing the sociomoral values and conflicts of a war-oriented society. It is interesting that the groundwork for such a value-free aesthetic is already being laid today, in growing experimentation in art without content, perhaps in anticipation of a world without conflict. A cult has developed around a new kind of cultural determinism,[12] which proposes that the technological form of a cultural expression determines its values rather than does its ostensibly meaningful content. Its clear implication is that there is no "good" or "bad" art, only that which is appropriate to its (technological) times and that which is not. Its cultural effect has been to promote circumstantial constructions and unplanned expressions; it denies to art the relevance of sequential logic. Its significance in this context is that it provides a working model of one kind of value-free culture we might reasonably anticipate in a world at peace.

So far as science is concerned, it might appear at first glance that a giant space-research program, the most promising among the proposed economic surrogates for war, might also serve as the basic stimulator of scientific research. The lack of fundamental organized social conflict inherent in space work, however, would rule it out as an adequate motivational substitute for war when applied to "pure" science. But it could no doubt sustain the broad range of *technological* activity that a space budget of military dimensions would require. A similarly scaled social-welfare program could provide a comparable impetus to low-keyed technological advances, especially in medicine, rationalized construction methods, educational psychology, etc. The eugenic substitute for the ecological function of war would also require continuing research in certain areas of the life sciences.

Apart from these partial substitutes for war, it must be

kept in mind that the momentum given to scientific progress by the great wars of the past century, and even more by the anticipation of World War III, is intellectually and materially enormous. It is our finding that if the war system were to end tomorrow this momentum is so great that the pursuit of scientific knowledge could reasonably be expected to go forward without noticeable diminution for perhaps two decades.[13] It would then continue, at a progressively decreasing tempo, for at least another two decades before the "bank account" of today's unresolved problems would become exhausted. By the standards of the questions we have learned to ask today, there would no longer be anything worth knowing still unknown; we cannot conceive, by definition, of the scientific questions to ask once those we can now comprehend are answered.

This leads unavoidably to another matter: the intrinsic value of the unlimited search for knowledge. We of course offer no independent value judgments here, but it is germane to point out that a substantial minority of scientific opinion feels that search to be circumscribed in any case. This opinion is itself a factor in considering the need for a substitute for the scientific function of war. For the record, we must also take note of the precedent that during long periods of human history, often covering thousands of years, in which no intrinsic social value was assigned to scientific progress, stable societies did survive and flourish. Although this could not have been possible in the modern industrial world, we cannot be certain it may not again be true in a future world at peace.

SUMMARY AND CONCLUSIONS

The Nature of War

WAR IS NOT, as is widely assumed, primarily an instrument of policy utilized by nations to extend or defend their expressed political values or their economic interests. On the contrary, it is itself the principal basis of organization on which all modern societies are constructed. The common proximate cause of war is the apparent interference of one nation with the aspirations of another. But at the root of all ostensible differences of national interest lie the dynamic requirements of the war system itself for periodic armed conflict. Readiness for war characterizes contemporary social systems more broadly than their economic and political structures, which it subsumes.

Economic analyses of the anticipated problems of transition to peace have not recognized the broad preeminence of war in the definition of social systems. The same is true, with rare and only partial exceptions, of model disarmament "scenarios." For this reason, the value of this previous work is limited to the mechanical aspects of transition. Certain features of these models may perhaps be applicable to a real situation of conversion to peace; this will depend on their compatibility with a substantive, rather than a procedural, peace plan. Such a plan can be developed only from the premise of full understanding of the nature of the war system it proposes to abolish, which in turn presupposes detailed comprehension of the functions the war system performs for society. It will require the construction of a detailed and feasible system of substitutes for those functions that are necessary to the stability and survival of human societies.

The Functions of War

The visible, military function of war requires no elucidation; it is not only obvious but also irrelevant to a transition to the condition of peace, in which it will by definition be superfluous. It is also subsidiary in social significance to the implied, nonmilitary functions of war; those critical to transition can be summarized in five principal groupings.

1. *Economic.* War has provided both ancient and modern societies with a dependable system for stabilizing and controlling national economies. No alternate method of control has yet been tested in a complex modern economy that has shown itself remotely comparable in scope or effectiveness.

2. *Political.* The permanent possibility of war is the foundation for stable government; it supplies the basis for general acceptance of political authority. It has enabled societies to maintain necessary class distinctions, and it has ensured the subordination of the citizen to the state, by virtue of the residual war powers inherent in the concept of nationhood. No modern political ruling group has successfully controlled its constituency after failing to sustain the continuing credibility of an external threat of war.

3. *Sociological.* War, through the medium of military institutions, has uniquely served societies, throughout the course of known history, as an indispensable controller of dangerous social dissidence and destructive antisocial ten-

dencies. As the most formidable of threats to life itself, and as the only one susceptible to mitigation by social organization alone, it has played another equally fundamental role: the war system has provided the machinery through which the motivational forces governing human behavior have been translated into binding social allegiance. It has thus ensured the degree of social cohesion necessary to the viability of nations. No other institution, or groups of institutions, in modern societies, has successfully served these functions.

4. *Ecological.* War has been the principal evolutionary device for maintaining a satisfactory ecological balance between gross human population and supplies available for its survival. It is unique to the human species.

5. *Cultural and Scientific.* War-orientation has determined the basic standards of value in the creative arts, and has provided the fundamental motivational source of scientific and technological progress. The concepts that the arts express values independent of their own forms and that the successful pursuit of knowledge has intrinsic social value have long been accepted in modern societies; the development of the arts and sciences during this period has been corollary to the parallel development of weaponry.

Substitutes for the Functions of War: Criteria

The foregoing functions of war are essential to the survival of the social systems we know today. With two possible exceptions they are also essential to any kind of stable social organization that might survive in a warless world. Discussion of the ways and means of transition to such a world are meaningless unless a) substitute institutions can be devised to fill these functions, or b) it can reasonably be hypothecated that the loss or partial loss of any one function need not destroy the viability of future societies.

Such substitute institutions and hypotheses must meet varying criteria. In general, they must be technically feasible, politically acceptable, and potentially credible to the members of the societies that adopt them. Specifically, they must be characterized as follows:

1. *Economic.* An acceptable economic surrogate for the war system will require the expenditure of resources for completely nonproductive purposes at a level comparable to that of the military expenditures otherwise demanded by the size and complexity of each society. Such a substitute system of apparent "waste" must be of a nature that will permit it to remain independent of the normal supply-demand economy; it must be subject to arbitrary political control.

2. *Political.* A viable political substitute for war must posit a generalized external menace to each society of a nature and degree sufficient to require the organization and acceptance of political authority.

3. *Sociological.* First, in the permanent absence of war, new institutions must be developed that will effectively control the socially destructive segments of societies. Second, for purposes of adapting the physical and psychological dynamics of human behavior to the needs of social organization, a credible substitute for war must generate an omnipresent and readily understood fear of personal destruction. This fear must be of a nature and degree sufficient to ensure adherence to societal values to the full extent that they are acknowledged to transcend the value of individual human life.

4. *Ecological.* A substitute for war in its function as the uniquely human system of population control must ensure

the survival, if not necessarily the improvement, of the species, in terms of its relation to environmental supply.

5. *Cultural and Scientific.* A surrogate for the function of war as the determinant of cultural values must establish a basis of sociomoral conflict of equally compelling force and scope. A substitute motivational basis for the quest for scientific knowledge must be similarly informed by a comparable sense of internal necessity.

Substitutes for the Functions of War: Models

The following substitute institutions, among others, have been proposed for consideration as replacements for the nonmilitary functions of war. That they may not have been originally set forth for that purpose does not preclude or invalidate their possible application here.

1. *Economic.* (a) A comprehensive social-welfare program, directed toward maximum improvement of general conditions of human life. (b) A giant open-end space-research program, aimed at unreachable targets. (c) A permanent, ritualized, ultra-elaborate disarmament inspection system, and variants of such a system.

2. *Political.* (a) An omnipresent, virtually omnipotent international police force. (b) An established and recognized extraterrestrial menace. (c) Massive global environmental pollution. (d) Fictitious alternate enemies.

3. *Sociological: Control function.* (a) Programs generally derived from the Peace Corps model. (b) A modern, sophisticated form of slavery. *Motivational function.* (a) Intensified environmental pollution. (b) New religions or other mythologies. (c) Socially oriented blood games. (d) Combination forms.

4. *Ecological.* A comprehensive program of applied eugenics.

5. *Cultural.* No replacement institution offered. *Scientific.* The secondary requirements of the space-research, social-welfare, and/or eugenics programs.

Substitutes for the Functions of War: Evaluation

The models listed above reflect only the beginning of the quest for substitute institutions for the functions of war, rather than a recapitulation of alternatives. It would be both premature and inappropriate, therefore, to offer final judgments on their applicability to a transition to peace and after. Furthermore, since the necessary but complex project of correlating the compatibility of proposed surrogates for different functions could be treated only in exemplary fashion at this time, we have elected to withhold such hypothetical correlations as were tested as statistically inadequate.[1]

Nevertheless, some tentative and cursory comments on these proposed functional "solutions" will indicate the scope of the difficulties involved in this area of peace planning.

Economic. The social-welfare model cannot be expected to remain outside the normal economy after the conclusion of its predominantly capital-investment phase; its value in this function can therefore be only temporary. The space-research substitute appears to meet both major criteria, and should be examined in greater detail, especially in respect to its probable effects on other war functions. "Elaborate inspection" schemes, although superficially attractive, are inconsistent with the basic premise of transition to peace. The "unarmed forces" variant, logistically similar, is subject to the same functional criticism as the general social-welfare model.

Political. Like the inspection-scheme surrogates, proposals for plenipotentiary international police are inherently incompatible with the ending of the war system. The "unarmed forces" variant, amended to include unlimited powers of economic sanction, might conceivably be expanded to constitute a credible external menace. Development of an acceptable threat from "outer space," presumably in conjunction with a space-research surrogate for economic control, appears unpromising in terms of credibility. The environmental-pollution model does not seem sufficiently responsive to immediate social control, except through arbitrary acceleration of current pollution trends; this in turn raises questions of political acceptability. New, less regressive, approaches to the creation of fictitious global "enemies" invite further investigation.

Sociological: Control function. Although the various substitutes proposed for this function that are modeled roughly on the Peace Corps appear grossly inadequate in potential scope, they should not be ruled out without further study. Slavery, in a technologically modern and conceptually euphemized form, may prove a more efficient and flexible institution in this area. *Motivational function.* Although none of the proposed substitutes for war as the guarantor of social allegiance can be dismissed out of hand, each presents serious and special difficulties. Intensified environmental threats may raise ecological dangers; mythmaking dissociated from war may no longer be politically feasible; purposeful blood games and rituals can far more readily be devised than implemented. An institution combining this function with the preceding one, based on, but not necessarily imitative of, the precedent of organized ethnic repression, warrants careful consideration.

Ecological. The only apparent problem in the application of an adequate eugenic substitute for war is that of timing; it cannot be effectuated until the transition to peace has been completed, which involves a serious temporary risk of ecological failure.

Cultural. No plausible substitute for this function of war has yet been proposed. It may be, however, that a basic cultural value-determinant is not necessary to the survival of a stable society. *Scientific.* The same might be said for the function of war as the prime mover of the search for knowledge. However, adoption of either a giant space-research program, a comprehensive social-welfare program, or a master program of eugenic control would provide motivation for limited technologies.

General Conclusions

It is apparent, from the foregoing, that no program or combination of programs yet proposed for a transition to peace has remotely approached meeting the comprehensive functional requirements of a world without war. Although one projected system for filling the economic function of war seems promising, similar optimism cannot be expressed in the equally essential political and sociological areas. The other major nonmilitary functions of war—ecological, cultural, scientific—raise very different problems, but it is at least possible that detailed programming of substitutes in these areas is not prerequisite to transition. More important, it is not enough to develop adequate but separate surrogates for the major war functions; they must be fully compatible and in no degree self-canceling.

Until such a unified program is developed, at least hypothetically, it is impossible for this or any other group to furnish meaningful answers to the questions originally presented to us. When asked how best to prepare for the advent of peace, we must first reply, as strongly as we can, that the war system cannot responsibly be allowed to disappear until 1) we know exactly what it is we plan to put in its place, and 2) we are certain, beyond reasonable doubt, that these substitute institutions will serve their purposes in terms of the survival and stability of society. It will then be time enough to develop methods for effectuating the transition; procedural programming must follow, not precede, substantive solutions.

Such solutions, if indeed they exist, will not be arrived at without a revolutionary revision of the modes of thought heretofore considered appropriate to peace research. That we have examined the fundamental questions involved from a dispassionate, value-free point of view should not imply that we do not appreciate the intellectual and emotional difficulties that must be overcome on all decision-making levels before these questions are generally acknowledged by others for what they are. They reflect, on an intellectual level, traditional emotional resistance to new (more lethal and thus more "shocking") forms of weaponry. The understated comment of then-Senator Hubert Humphrey on the publication of *On Thermonuclear War* is still very much to the point: "New thoughts, particularly those which appear to contradict current assumptions, are always painful for the mind to contemplate."

Nor, simply because we have not discussed them, do we minimize the massive reconciliation of conflicting interests which domestic as well as international agreement on proceeding toward genuine peace presupposes. This factor was excluded from the purview of our assignment, but we would be remiss if we failed to take it into account. Although no insuperable obstacle lies in the path of reaching such general agreements, formidable short-term private-group and general-class interest in maintaining the war system is well established and widely recognized. The resistance to peace stemming from such interest is only tangential, in the long run, to the basic functions of war, but it will not be easily overcome, in this country or elsewhere. Some observers, in fact, believe that it cannot be overcome at all in our time, that the price of peace is, simply, too high. This bears on our overall conclusions to the extent that timing in the transference to substitute institutions may often be the critical factor in their political feasibility.

It is uncertain, at this time, whether peace will ever be possible. It is far more questionable, by the objective standard of continued social survival rather than that of emotional pacifism, that it would be desirable even if it were demonstrably attainable. The war system, for all its subjective repugnance to important sections of "public opinion," has demonstrated its effectiveness since the beginning of recorded history; it has provided the basis for the development of many impressively durable civilizations, including that which is dominant today. It has consistently provided unambiguous social priorities. It is, on the whole, a known quantity. A viable system of peace, assuming that the great and complex questions of substitute institutions raised in this Report are both soluble and solved, would still constitute a venture into the unknown, with the inevitable risks attendant on the unforeseen, however small and however well hedged.

Government decision-makers tend to choose peace over war whenever a real option exists, because it usually appears to be the "safer" choice. Under most immediate circumstances they are likely to be right. But in terms of long-range social stability, the opposite is true. At our present state of knowledge and reasonable inference, it is the war system that must be identified with stability, the peace system with social speculation, however justifiable the speculation may appear, in terms of subjective moral or emotional values. A nuclear physicist once remarked, in respect to a possible disarmament agreement: "If we could change the world into a world in which no weapons could be made, that would be stabilizing. But agreements we can expect with the Soviets would be destabilizing."[2] The qualification and the bias are equally irrelevant; *any* condition of genuine total peace, however achieved, would be destabilizing until proved otherwise.

If it were necessary at this moment to opt irrevocably for the retention or for the dissolution of the war system, common prudence would dictate the former course. But it is not yet necessary, late as the hour appears. And more factors must eventually enter the war-peace equation than even the most determined search for alternative institutions for the functions of war can be expected to reveal. One group of such factors has been given only passing mention in this Report; it centers around the possible obsolescence of the war system itself. We have noted, for instance, the limitations of the war system in filling its ecological function and the declining importance of this aspect of war. It by no means stretches the imagination to visualize comparable developments which may compromise the efficacy of war as, for example, an economic controller or as an organizer of social allegiance. This kind of possibility, however remote, serves as a reminder that all calculations of contingency not only involve the weighing of one group of risks against another, but require a respectful allowance for error on both sides of the scale.

A more expedient reason for pursuing the investigation

of alternate ways and means to serve the current functions of war is narrowly political. It is possible that one or more major sovereign nations may arrive, through ambiguous leadership, at a position in which a ruling administrative class may lose control of basic public opinion or of its ability to rationalize a desired war. It is not hard to imagine, in such circumstance, a situation in which such governments may feel forced to initiate serious full-scale disarmament proceedings (perhaps provoked by "accidental" nuclear explosions), and that such negotiations may lead to the actual disestablishment of military institutions. As our Report has made clear, this could be catastrophic. It seems evident that, in the event an important part of the world is suddenly plunged without sufficient warning into an inadvertent peace, even partial and inadequate preparation for the possibility may be better than none. The difference could even be critical. The models considered in the preceding chapter, both those that seem promising and those that do not, have one positive feature in common—an inherent flexibility of phasing. And despite our strictures against knowingly proceeding into peace-transition procedures without thorough substantive preparation, our government must nevertheless be ready to move in this direction with whatever limited resources of planning are on hand at the time—if circumstances so require. An arbitrary all-or-nothing approach is no more realistic in the development of contingency peace programming than it is anywhere else.

But the principal cause for concern over the continuing effectiveness of the war system, and the more important reason for hedging with peace planning, lies in the backwardness of current war-system programming. Its controls have not kept pace with the technological advances it has made possible. Despite its unarguable success to date, even in this era of unprecedented potential in mass destruction, it continues to operate largely on a laissez-faire basis. To the best of our knowledge, no serious quantified studies have ever been conducted to determine, for example:

—optimum levels of armament production, for purposes of economic control, at any given series of chronological points and under any given relationship between civilian production and consumption patterns;

—correlation factors between draft recruitment policies and mensurable social dissidence;

—minimum levels of population destruction necessary to maintain war-threat credibility under varying political conditions;

—optimum cyclical frequency of "shooting" wars under varying circumstances of historical relationship.

These and other war-function factors are fully susceptible to analysis by today's computer-based systems,[3] but they have not been so treated; modern analytical techniques have up to now been relegated to such aspects of the ostensible functions of war as procurement, personnel deployment, weapons analysis, and the like. We do not disparage these types of application, but only deplore their lack of utilization to greater capacity in attacking problems of broader scope. Our concern for efficiency in this context is not aesthetic, economic, or humanistic. It stems from the axiom that no system can long survive at either input or output levels that consistently or substantially deviate from an optimum range. As their data grow increasingly sophisticated, the war system and its functions are increasingly endangered by such deviations.

Our final conclusion, therefore, is that it will be necessary for our government to plan in depth for two general contingencies. The first, and lesser, is the possibility of a viable general peace; the second is the successful continuation of the war system. In our view, careful preparation for the possibility of peace should be extended, not because we take the position that the end of war would necessarily be desirable, if it is in fact possible, but because it may be thrust upon us in some form whether we are ready for it or not. Planning for rationalizing and quantifying the war system, on the other hand, to ensure the effectiveness of its major stabilizing functions, is not only more promising in respect to anticipated results, but is essential; we can no longer take for granted that it will continue to serve our purposes well merely because it always has. The objective of government policy in regard to war and peace, in this period of uncertainty, must be to preserve maximum options. The recommendations which follow are directed to this end.

RECOMMENDATIONS

(1) We propose the establishment, under executive order of the President, of a permanent War/Peace Research Agency, empowered and mandated to execute the programs described in (2) and (3) below. This agency (a) will be provided with nonaccountable funds sufficient to implement its responsibilities and decisions at its own discretion, and (b) will have authority to preempt and utilize, without restriction, any and all facilities of the executive branch of the government in pursuit of its objectives. It will be organized along the lines of the National Security Council, except that none of its governing, executive, or operating personnel will hold other public office or governmental responsibility. Its directorate will be drawn from the broadest practicable spectrum of scientific disciplines, humanistic studies, applied creative arts, operating technologies, and otherwise unclassified professional occupations. It will be responsible solely to the President, or to other officers of government temporarily deputized by him. Its operations will be governed entirely by its own rules of procedure. Its authority will expressly include the unlimited right to withhold information on its activities and its decisions, from anyone except the President, whenever it deems such secrecy to be in the public interest.

(2) THE FIRST OF THE WAR/PEACE RESEARCH AGENCY'S two principal responsibilities will be to determine all that can

be known, including what can reasonably be inferred in terms of relevant statistical probabilities, that may bear on an eventual transition to a general condition of peace. The findings in this Report may be considered to constitute the beginning of this study and to indicate its orientation; detailed records of the investigations and findings of the Special Study Group on which this Report is based, will be furnished the agency, along with whatever clarifying data the agency deems necessary. This aspect of the agency's work will hereinafter be referred to as "Peace Research."

The Agency's Peace Research activities will necessarily include, but not be limited to, the following:

(a) The creative development of possible substitute institutions for the principal nonmilitary functions of war.

(b) The careful matching of such institutions against the criteria summarized in this Report, as refined, revised, and extended by the agency.

(c) The testing and evaluation of substitute institutions, for acceptability, feasibility, and credibility, against hypothecated transitional and postwar conditions; the testing and evaluation of the effects of the anticipated atrophy of certain unsubstituted functions.

(d) The development and testing of the correlativity of multiple substitute institutions, with the eventual objective of establishing a comprehensive program of compatible war substitutes suitable for a planned transition to peace, if and when this is found to be possible and subsequently judged desirable by appropriate political authorities.

(e) The preparation of a wide-ranging schedule of partial, uncorrelated, crash programs of adjustment suitable for reducing the dangers of an unplanned transition to peace effected by *force majeure.*

Peace Research methods will include but not be limited to, the following:

(a) The comprehensive interdisciplinary application of historical, scientific, technological, and cultural data.

(b) The full utilization of modern methods of mathematical modeling, analogical analysis, and other, more sophisticated, quantitative techniques in process of development that are compatible with computer programming.

(c) The heuristic "peace games" procedures developed during the course of its assignment by the Special Study Group, and further extensions of this basic approach to the testing of institutional functions.

(3) THE WAR/PEACE RESEARCH AGENCY'S other principal responsibility will be "War Research." Its fundamental objective will be to ensure the continuing viability of the war system to fulfill its essential nonmilitary functions for as long as the war system is judged necessary to or desirable for the survival of society. To achieve this end, the War Research groups within the agency will engage in the following activities:

(a) *Quantification of existing application of the nonmilitary functions of war.* Specific determinations will include, but not be limited to: 1) the gross amount and the net proportion of nonproductive military expenditures since World War II assignable to the need for war as an economic stabilizer; 2) the amount and proportion of military expenditures and destruction of life, property, and natural resources during this period assignable to the need for war as an instrument for political control; 3) similar figures, to the extent that they can be separately arrived at, assignable to the need for war to maintain social cohesiveness; 4) levels of recruitment and expenditures on the draft and other forms of personnel deployment attributable to the need for military institutions to control social disaffection; 5) the statistical relationship of war casualties to world food supplies; 6) the correlation of military actions and expenditures with cultural activities and scientific advances (including necessarily, the development of mensurable standards in these areas).

(b) *Establishment of a priori modern criteria for the execution of the nonmilitary functions of war.* These will include, but not be limited to: 1) calculation of minimum and optimum ranges of military expenditure required, under varying hypothetical conditions, to fulfill these several functions, separately and collectively; 2) determination of minimum and optimum levels of destruction of life, property, and natural resources prerequisite to the credibility of external threat essential to the political and motivational functions; 3) development of a negotiable formula governing the relationship between military recruitment and training policies and the exigencies of social control.

(c) *Reconciliation of these criteria with prevailing economic, political, sociological, and ecological limitations.* The ultimate object of this phase of War Research is to rationalize the heretofore informal operations of the war system. It should provide practical working procedures through which responsible governmental authority may resolve the following war-function problems, among others, under any given circumstances: 1) how to determine the optimum quantity, nature, and timing of military expenditures to ensure a desired degree of economic control; 2) how to organize the recruitment, deployment, and ostensible use of military personnel to ensure a desired degree of acceptance of authorized social values; 3) how to compute on a short-term basis, the nature and extent of the loss of life and other resources which should be suffered and/or inflicted during any single outbreak of hostilities to achieve a desired degree of internal political authority and social allegiance; 4) how to project, over extended periods, the nature and quality of overt warfare which must be planned and budgeted to achieve a desired degree of contextual stability for the same purpose; factors to be determined must include frequency of occurrence, length of phase, intensity of physical destruction, extensiveness of geographical involvement, and optimum mean loss of life; 5) how to extrapolate accurately from the foregoing, for ecological purposes, the continuing effect of the war system, over such extended cycles, on population pressures, and to adjust the planning of casualty rates accordingly.

War Research procedures will necessarily include, but not be limited to, the following:

(a) The collation of economic, military, and other relevant data into uniform terms, permitting the reversible translation of heretofore discrete categories of information.[1]

(b) The development and application of appropriate forms of cost-effectiveness analysis suitable for adapting such new constructs to computer terminology, programming, and projection.[2]

(c) Extension of the "war games" methods of systems testing to apply, as a quasi-adversary proceeding, to the nonmilitary functions of war.[3]

(4) SINCE BOTH PROGRAMS of the War/Peace Research Agency will share the same purpose—to maintain governmental freedom of choice in respect to war and peace until the direction of social survival is no longer in doubt—it is

of the essence of this proposal that the agency be constituted without limitation of time. Its examination of existing
and proposed institutions will be self-liquidating when its
own function shall have been superseded by the historical
developments it will have, at least in part, initiated.

NOTES

SECTION 1
1. *The Economic and Social Consequences of Disarmament: U.S. Reply to the Inquiry of the Secretary-General of the United Nations* (Washington, D.C.: USGPO, June 1964), pp. 8–9.
2. Herman Kahn, *Thinking About the Unthinkable* (New York: Horizon, 1962), p. 35.
3. Robert S. McNamara, in an address before the American Society of Newspaper Editors, in Montreal, P.Q., Canada, 18 May 1966.
4. Alfred North Whitehead, in "The Anatomy of Some Scientific Ideas," included in *The Aims of Education* (New York: Macmillan, 1929).
5. At Ann Arbor, Michigan, 16 June 1962.
6. Louis J. Halle, "Peace in Our Time? Nuclear Weapons as a Stabilizer," *The New Republic* (28 December 1963).

SECTION 2
1. Kenneth E. Boulding, "The World War Industry as an Economic Problem," in Emile Benoit and Kenneth E. Boulding (eds.), *Disarmament and the Economy* (New York: Harper & Row, 1963).
2. McNamara, in ASNE Montreal address cited.
3. *Report of the Committee on the Economic Impact of Defense and Disarmament* (Washington: USGPO, July 1965).
4. Sumner M. Rosen, "Disarmament and the Economy," *War/Peace Report* (March 1966).

SECTION 3
1. *Vide* William D. Grampp, "False Fears of Disarmament," *Harvard Business Review* (Jan.-Feb. 1964), for a concise example of this reasoning.
2. Seymour Melman, "The Cost of Inspection for Disarmament," in Benoit and Boulding, *op. cit.*

SECTION 5
1. Arthur I. Waskow, *Toward the Unarmed Forces of the United States* (Washington: Institute for Policy Studies, 1966), p. 9. (This is the

unabridged edition of the text of a report and proposal prepared for a seminar of strategists and Congressmen in 1965; it was later given limited distribution among other persons engaged in related projects.)

2. David T. Bazelon, "The Politics of the Paper Economy," *Commentary* (November 1962), p. 409.

3. *The Economic Impact of Disarmament* (Washington: USGPO, January 1962).

4. David T. Bazelon, "The Scarcity Makers," *Commentary* (October 1962), p. 298.

5. Frank Pace, Jr., in an address before the American Bankers' Association, September 1957.

6. A random example, taken in this case from a story by David Deitch in the New York *Herald Tribune* (9 February 1966).

7. *Vide* L. Gumplowicz, in *Geschichte der Staatstheorien* (Innsbruck: Wagner, 1905) and earlier writings.

8. K. Fischer, *Das Militär* (Zurich: Steinmetz Verlag, 1932), pp. 42–43.

9. The obverse of this phenomenon is responsible for the principal combat problem of present-day infantry officers: the unwillingness of otherwise "trained" troops to fire at an enemy close enough to be recognizable as an individual rather than simply as a target.

10. Herman Kahn, *On Thermonuclear War* (Princeton, N.J.: Princeton University Press, 1960), p. 42.

11. John D. Williams, "The Nonsense about Safe Driving," *Fortune* (September 1958).

12. *Vide* most recently K. Lorenz, in *Das Sogenannte Böse: zur Naturgeschichte der Aggression* (Vienna: G. Borotha-Schoeler Verlag, 1964).

13. Beginning with Herbert Spencer and his contemporaries, but largely ignored for nearly a century.

14. As in recent draft-law controversy, in which the issue of selective deferment of the culturally privileged is often carelessly equated with the preservation of the biologically "fittest."

15. G. Bouthoul, in *La Guerre* (Paris: Presses universitaires de France, 1953) and many other more detailed studies. The useful concept of "polemology," for the study of war as an independent discipline, is his, as is the notion of "demographic relaxation," the sudden temporary decline in the rate of population increase after major wars.

16. This seemingly premature statement is supported by one of our own test studies. But it hypothecates both the stabilizing of world population growth and the institution of fully adequate environmental controls. Under these two conditions, the probability of the permanent elimination of involuntary global famine is 68 percent by 1976 and 95 percent by 1981.

SECTION 6

1. This round figure is the median taken from our computations, which cover varying contingencies, but it is sufficient for the purpose of general discussion.
2. But less misleading than the more elegant traditional metaphor, in which war expenditures are referred to as the "ballast" of the economy but which suggest incorrect quantitative relationships.
3. Typical in generality, scope, and rhetoric. We have not used any published program as a model; similarities are unavoidably coincidental rather than tendentious.
4. *Vide* the reception of a "Freedom Budget for all Americans," proposed by A. Philip Randolph *et al;* it is a ten-year plan, estimated by its sponsors to cost $185 billion.
5. Waskow, *op. cit.*
6. By several current theorists, most extensively and effectively by Robert R. Harris in *The Real Enemy,* an unpublished doctoral dissertation made available to this study.
7. In ASNE Montreal address cited.
8. *The Tenth Victim.*
9. For an examination of some of its social implications, see Seymour Rubenfeld, *Family of Outcasts: A New Theory of Delinquency* (New York: Free Press, 1965).
10. As in Nazi Germany; this type of "ideological" ethnic repression, directed to specific sociological ends, should not be confused with traditional economic exploitation, as of Negroes in the U.S., South Africa, etc.
11. By teams of experimental biologists in Massachusetts, Michigan, and California, as well as in Mexico and the U.S.S.R. Preliminary test applications are scheduled in Southeast Asia, in countries not yet announced.
12. Expressed in the writings of H. Marshall McLuhan, in *Understanding Media: The Extensions of Man* (New York: McGraw-Hill, 1964) and elsewhere.
13. This rather optimistic estimate was derived by plotting a three-

dimensional distribution of three arbitrarily defined variables; the macro-structural, relating to the extension of knowledge beyond the capacity of conscious experience; the organic, dealing with the manifestations of terrestrial life as inherently comprehensible; and the infra-particular, covering the subconceptual requirements of natural phenomena. Values were assigned to the known and unknown in each parameter, tested against data from earlier chronologies, and modified heuristically until predictable correlations reached a useful level of accuracy. "Two decades" means, in this case, 20.6 years, with a standard deviation of only 1.8 years. (An incidental finding, not pursued to the same degree of accuracy, suggests a greatly accelerated resolution of issues in the biological sciences after 1972.)

SECTION 7

1. Since they represent an examination of too small a percentage of the eventual options, in terms of "multiple mating," the subsystem we developed for this application. But an example will indicate how one of the most frequently recurring correlation problems—chronological phasing—was brought to light in this way. One of the first combinations tested showed remarkably high coefficients of compatibility, on a *post hoc* static basis, but no variations of timing, using a thirty-year transition module, permitted even marginal synchronization. The combination was thus disqualified. This would not rule out the possible adequacy of combinations using modifications of the same factors, however, since minor variations in a proposed final condition may have disproportionate effects on phasing.

2. Edward Teller, quoted in *War/Peace Report* (December 1964).

3. E.g., the highly publicized "Delphi technique" and other, more sophisticated procedures. A new system, especially suitable for institutional analysis, was developed during the course of this study in order to hypothecate mensurable "peace games"; a manual of this system is being prepared and will be submitted for general distribution among appropriate agencies. For older, but still useful, techniques, see Norman C. Dalkey's *Games and Simulations* (Santa Monica, Calif.: Rand, 1964).

SECTION 8

1. A primer-level example of the obvious and long overdue need for such translation is furnished by Kahn (in *Thinking About the*

Unthinkable, p. 102). Under the heading "Some Awkward Choices" he compares four hypothetical policies: a certain loss of $3,000; a .1 chance of loss of $300,000; a .01 chance of loss of $30,000,000; and a .001 chance of loss of $3,000,000,000. A government decision-maker would "very likely" choose in that order. But what if "lives are at stake rather than dollars"? Kahn suggests that the order of choice would be reversed, although current experience does not support this opinion. Rational war research can and must make it possible to express, without ambiguity, lives in terms of dollars and vice versa; the choices need not be, and cannot be, "awkward."

2. Again, an overdue extension of an obvious application of techniques up to now limited to such circumscribed purposes as improving kill–ammunition ratios, determining local choice between precision and saturation bombing, and other minor tactical, and occasionally strategic, ends. The slowness of Rand, I.D.A., and other responsible analytic organizations to extend cost-effectiveness and related concepts beyond early-phase applications has already been widely remarked on and criticized elsewhere.

3. The inclusion of institutional factors in war-game techniques has been given some rudimentary consideration in the Hudson Institute's *Study for Hypothetical Narratives for Use in Command and Control Systems Planning* (by William Pfaff and Edmund Stillman; Final report published 1963). But here, as with other war and peace studies to date, what has blocked the logical extension of new analytic techniques has been a general failure to understand and properly evaluate the nonmilitary functions of war.

AFTERWORD
BY THE AUTHOR

NOW THAT YOU HAVE finished reading this book, there is no need for me to try and explain the substance of some of its prose. But I would like to let you know why it was written as it was and what may account for its apparent resilience.

The book is, of course, a satirical hoax—a fact not so obvious in 1967 when it first appeared and, disturbingly, still lost on some people today. The targets of the book then were military-supported "think tanks," whose pseudo-scientific assertions were taken quite seriously by people in the defense department and military industries. In that vein, each sentence of the book alone might seem quite reasonable and even astute—but like the think-tank jargon it lampoons, the book's cumulative "logic" eventually arrives at outrageous conclusions. Another objective of the book was to serve as a warning that a transition from a war economy to a peace economy would not be easy, a point that appears all the more pertinent today.

My desire was for the *Report* to provoke debate, and so it has in varying degrees. When the book first appeared my co-conspirators and I, by implication and indirect suggestion, maintained an ongoing dispute: Was Iron Mountain some kind of government-related report, or was it satirical fiction—and, if so, who wrote it? This led to a lively discussion of the issues and problems taken up by the book, even in quarters where it was understood to be fictional.

After a while, it seemed unnecessary to continue going along with this who-done-it game, so in an early 1972 *New York Times Book Review* I "confessed" to having written the *Report*. Oddly enough, this "confession" came after a number of real government reports (e.g., the *Pentagon Papers* and the *Pax Americana*) had already been leaked—sounding more like parodies of *Iron Mountain* than the reverse.

Iron Mountain was generally unavailable in the 1980s in the U.S., or so I had thought. I began to receive a growing number of requests for the book, and to my surprise found that several were from far-right groups now calling themselves militias. Their interest in *Iron Mountain*—aside from their being apparently unable to recognize or understand satire—was in identifying, either pro or con, with some of the assertions of the book's "Special Study Group." It took me a while to realize that not only were they serious, but that copies of the book had somehow become available to them.

In 1990 I discovered that *Iron Mountain* was being advertised and disseminated in bootleg editions by a number of ultraright groups and others including Liberty Lobby, publishers of *Spotlight;* the *Noontide Press;* and the Institute for Historical Review, associated with the proposition that the Holocaust never took place. I took legal action against them for copyright infringement: Their defense was primarily that the book was in fact a government document, not subject to copyright.

The book was pulled from print and the remaining copies turned over to me. But did I win? I would like to think so. I have no regrets in having written the book: You can never foresee how something you write might be misused, and I hope that the book can serve today as a warning against superficial logic. And if I'm given reason to believe that readers are able to find some useful ideas in the mixture that might help lead to some real program for a real peace, that will do nicely.

L.C.L.
November 1995

"THE IRON MOUNTAIN AFFAIR"

"Report" on Peace Gets Mixed Views
Some See Book as Hoax, Others Take it Seriously
By John Leo

THE BOOK is variously described as "a harmless sub-terfuge," "a hair-raising analysis," "the sinister work of a sick mind," and "a serious fraud."

It is "Report From Iron Mountain: On the Possibility and Desirability of Peace," published last week by the Dial Press and described as a suppressed Government report arguing that the world would face an unparalleled catas-trophe if the world ever achieved peace.

The report states that war and war preparations are politically, psychologically and culturally indispensable to world stability. Its unidentified authors conclude that "lasting peace, while not theoretically impossible, is prob-ably unattainable; even if it could be achieved it would almost certainly not be in the best interests of a stable soci-ety to achieve it."

"If it's authentic, it's an enormous roaring scandal," said Lee Rainwater, a sociologist at Washington University in St. Louis. "If it's caricature, it's a brilliant job. There are people who really think like that."

Richard Baron, president of Dial, says the report is authentic. Harold Hayes, editor of Esquire magazine, which is publishing a 28,000-word condensation of the book in its December issue, says he accepts Dial's assurances on trustworthiness. But generally publishers, reviewers and Government officials who have seen advance copies consider the book a hoax. "To our knowledge no such special study group ever existed," said a press spokesman for the State Department's Arms Control and Disarmament Agency. "But it's cleverly done, and who ever did it obviously has an appreciable grasp of the disciplines involved." However, no advance reviewer has flatly labeled the book fiction.

The book carries an introduction by Leonard C. Lewin, a New York freelance writer, who states that "John Doe," a professor of social science from a large Middle Western university secretly passed the manuscript to him last winter.

Doe is described as one of the 15 members of a special Government study group convened at "Iron Mountain, N.Y." from 1963 to 1966 to produce the report for an unspecified Federal agency.

Iron Mountain is described in the book as being near the city of Hudson, N.Y., apparently a reference to the Hudson Institute, the think tank where "war games" and studies on life in the future are developed under the direction of Herman Kahn for Government and private agencies.

"We had nothing to do with it," said Mr. Kahn. "It sounds nutty to me—either a practical joke or something sinister. No analysis of conversion to the peacetime that I've seen has suggested such radical measures."

Slavery and Poison

In a cold, flat style—described by some readers as "perfect bureaucratese"—the report suggests that if the social cohesion brought by war is allowed to disappear without extensive planning, the world may have to introduce "a sophisticated form of slavery," invent enemies from outside the planet, or deliberately poison the atmosphere "in a politically acceptable manner."

The book suggests that some flying saucer incidents may have been Government attempts to test public responses to outside enemies.

The end of war, it said, would necessarily mean the end of the nation-state, and would introduce world government and the need for wasteful spending on a large scale, perhaps through an unlimited space program aimed at reaching unreachable points in space.

"I disagree that the end of war would wrench and destroy the nation-state system," said Arthur I. Waskow of the Institute for Policy Studies in Washington. "But this is the best case I've ever read on the other side. It gives me very tough arguments to answer."

Mr. Waskow said that if the report is authentic it would probably have come from the Bureau of the Budget or the Central Intelligence Agency. He added that he was surprised to see one of his privately circulated reports mentioned in the Iron Mountain book.

"As far as I know, only about 60 people in Washington ever saw my report. If it's a hoax, it must involve somebody high up."

Many analysts believe that the report reflects a grasp of the Washington scene as well as an understanding of social psychology, ecology, economics and sociology that is beyond the ability of most satirists.

Publishing figures who asked not to be identified said that the Harvard economist John Kenneth Galbraith had such qualifications. Under the pseudonym Mark Eparnay, he has written several political satires, including "The

McLandless Dimension," which appeared in Esquire several years ago.

Galbraith to Review

He is reviewing the Iron Mountain book under the pseudonym "Herschel McLandless" for Book World, a weekly supplement to The Chicago Tribune and The Washington Post. Book World is edited by Byron Dobell, who was a managing editor at Esquire until recent weeks.

When asked if he was reviewing his own book for Book World, he said: "That would be unethical. Is the Times suggesting I acted unethically?"

He added that he couldn't say whether he had a hand in writing Iron Mountain because "some things are so far removed from reality that they can't be commented on."

According to the book's introduction, the study group met between 1963 and 1966. That was when a study was made by the Washington Center of Foreign Policy Research for the Arms Control and Disarmament Agency. The study, published July 10, 1966, said President Johnson's disarmament plan could upset world stability instead of promoting peace.

News of War and Peace You're Not Ready For
By Herschel McLandress

THREE QUESTIONS ARE RAISED by the unauthorized publication of this deeply controversial document. The first concerns its authenticity. The second concerns the validity of the several considerations that caused one of the authors, on his own motion and in violation of his implicit oath, to release it for publication, and the collateral question of whether, within the genially accepted ethical framework of the free enterprise system, Dial Press was justified in publishing it. The third question concerns the empirical-theoretical validity of the conclusions.

As to the authenticity of the document, it happens that this reviewer can speak to the full extent of his personal authority and credibility. In the summer of 1963 I received a telephone call from a scientist friend—a well-known astronomer, physicist and communications theorist. This was on the eve of my departure for a month-long seminar on modern psychometric theory at the Villa Cerbolloni in Italy. I was asked to attend a meeting a week hence to discuss a project of high national influence at Iron Mountain in upstate New York. I knew the place well, for Iron Mountain was the working headquarters of the committee of selection set up by the Chase Manhattan Bank which, after establishing working criteria, designated the nucleus of bank executives to be protected in the event of nuclear attack. But the Italian meetings were also of high urgency and had been planned long in advance. Accordingly, I was forced to decline. I was then instructed to keep the invitation strictly confidential. On two subsequent occasions I was consulted by the psychiatrist and specialist on the relationship between individual and group behavior whom, more than incidentally, I recommended to take my place. I have concluded that I do not now violate any controlling ethical precepts in relating this history. As far as I personally am concerned, it leaves no doubt as to the credibly of this document. The public would not be more assured had I written it myself.

As to the ethics of the author in releasing it I do have grave reservations. In a democracy there must be the fullest and frankest and freest discussion of all matters of fundamental public concern. On this issue there can be no compromise; it is what makes us a free country and a leader of what the Secretary of State has called the Free World. But the precise timing of such democratic discussion is of the highest importance. As a matter of elementary prudence, it should not occur before the public is psychologically conditioned to the issues. Otherwise there is danger that anger, hysteria or immature and unsophisticated moral indignation will replace conditioned perception of fundamental truth. The authors of this document rightly saw that the public was not yet prepared for a rational discussion of the indispensability of war for the preservation of the modern social fabric. For generations there has been intense socially unscientific conditioning to the opposite view. This cannot be quickly offset.

In recent years, it is true that at the Institutes of International Relations at the leading universities, at the Hudson

Institute and Rand and in seminars for the discussion of peace and international conciliation, there has been analysis of what, suggestively, is still called the unthinkable. New scholarly disciplines have come into being, schooled in systems analysis and game theory, which are capable of considering objectively the relative social advantages and disadvantages of differing levels of annihilation. But the public impact of this work has so far been limited. In consequence, the public is not now prepared to deal rationally with the kind of discussion this report will provoke. The member of the Special Study Group who decided upon its premature release bears heavy responsibility for his action. At an absolute minimum it should first have been discussed at strictly off-the-record meetings with responsible and conservative Congressional leaders, key private citizen in New York and sympathetic editors. Only then should the public have been brought into the debate.

The third question concerns the conclusions. Here one can be brief, for these, without question, are thoroughly sound. This was inevitable. The reaction to war, hitherto, has been moralistic, emotional and even oratorical. This is the first study of its social role to be grounded firmly on modern social science and buttressed by modern empirical techniques as extended and refined by computer technology. That it should find that war provides the only dependable system "for stabilizing and controlling" national economies; that it is the source of the public authority that makes stable government possible; that it is indispensable sociologically for the control of "dangerous social dissidence and destructive antisocial tendencies"; that it serves an indispensable Malthusian function; and it has long "provided the fundamental motivational source of scientific and technological progress" is only what was to be expected from any soundly conceived scientific application of modern team research.

Many of us, no doubt, would have stressed additional advantages. In recent times it has been my privilege to draw attention to what is now being called, perhaps a bit awkwardly, the anticipatory retrospective national guilt complex as an important motivational factor growing out of war. It deserves a word of explanation. In wartime the disruption of family life patterns, combat morbidity and mortality, and in those countries suffering actual combat or air attack, destruction of personal property, civilian casualties, defoliation of landscape and malnutrition have caused Perceptive Thought Leaders who previously had been relatively indifferent to the well-being of others to anticipate the guilt feelings of the community when, in postwar years, it comes to reflect on how some individuals and subcultures have suffered more than others for the common good. Accordingly, while the war continues these PTLs address themselves to planning measures of amelioration—full employment, G. I. Bills of Rights, homes for heroes, international peacekeeping arrangements, physical reconstruction, new power dams and irrigation projects, and such international relief efforts as those of Herbert Hoover and UNRRA—which will act as a social solvent for guilt by providing those afflicted with a compensating economic or moral gain. The years immediately following any war, as a result, are ones of no slight social progress on various national and international fronts. This progress only comes to an end as the feeling of war guilt is exorcised and normal psychological patterns of thought are restored.

But this is a detail. As I would put my personal repute behind the authenticity of this document, so I would testify to the validity of its conclusions. My reservations relate only to the wisdom of releasing it to an obviously unconditioned public.

Peace—It Could Be Horrible
By Eliot Fremont-Smith

"REPORT FROM IRON MOUNTAIN" purports to be a secret think tank report prepared between 1963 and 1966 for an anonymous high-level interagency Government committee by an interdisciplinary civilian Special Study Group (also anonymous) on the implications of world peace for the future stability of American society with recommendations to maximize present and future Government policy options.

The report was supposedly delivered to Leonard C. Lewin by John Doe, one of the 15 members of the Special Study Group, in an act of conscience: the report's findings are, he is said to have said, so revolutionary and far-reaching that they should be made available for public discussion.

It is, of course, a hoax—but what a hoax!—a parody so elaborate and ingenious and, in fact, so substantively original, acute, interesting and horrifying, that it will receive serious attention regardless of its origin. No one has yet admitted its true origin, and my calling it a hoax must be taken as pure assertion—though it is based, I think, on clear and ample internal evidence.

134

Who Did It?

There has been much speculation about the identity of the parodist: John Kenneth Galbraith has been mentioned, so have Kenneth Boulding and other known strategic thinkers, on the questionable assumption that only an insider could have done it. But granted genius and a will, anyone moderately familiar with the published strategic studies of the Rand Corporation, Herman Kahn's Hudson Institute (It is maintained that "Iron Mountain" is near Hudson, N.Y.), etc., could have done it. My own guess is that the report is the work of Mr. Lewin himself, perhaps with some consultative aid from the editors of Monocle magazine. Not incidentally, Mr. Lewin put together the splendid collection of political satire, "A Treasury of American Political Humor" (1964), a fact that is—again, not incidentally—omitted from this book.

In any case, "Report From Iron Mountain" is a shocker. Its basic argument is that social stability is, and has always been, based on a war system; and that, contrary to the "incorrect assumption that war, as an institution, is subordinate to the social system it is believed to serve, . . . war itself is the basic social system." This is presented with intriguing reference to a variety of important economic, political, sociological, ecological, cultural and scientific "functions" of war (or the threat of war or preparedness for war).

The focus of the report, however, is on how social stability might be maintained in the unlikely but "not theoretically impossible" event that a lasting peace (world disarmament is subsumed in the term) is thrust upon us; on how the most crucial functions of the war system could be adequately transferred to a peace system.

The prospect the report outlines is truly Orwellian. It

includes planned but credible "threats" from an "enemy," a space research program that is deliberately costly (and not subject to open market fluctuations) and deliberately unproductive, programmed air and water pollution, computer-controlled procreation, the reintroduction of slavery and possibly of ritual-killing and genocide. Since the effectiveness of some of these methods would be severely compromised and even nullified by public awareness of their deliberate implementation, they must be kept secret.

The War System

Clearly, the report concludes, peace is not desirable, either for social stability or for the survival of the species. Yet evidence is suggested that the war system may be breaking down, willy-nilly. The report therefore explores the application of some of its findings to maintaining the war system against the possibilities of peace, should that be determined the most desirable option.

"Report From Iron Mountain" is a hoax, a biting conceptual and stylistic parody of modern, sophisticated think tank speculation. But it is a parody with a difference, more suggestive and disturbing than funny—in fact, hardly funny at all. It is ridiculous; it is also a telling and oddly lucid outline of some important theoretical problems of peace and war that have rarely been admitted to in public or in private.

Hoax or Horror? A Book That Shook White House

There can be no peace, but endless war may be good for the U.S. anyway—that is the conclusion reported in a volume causing a severe case of jitters in official Washington. Reason: The book purports to be based on a secret, Government-financed study by top experts. Some say it is grimly serious. Others call it leg-pulling satire. Whatever the truth, it is something of a sensation in high places

D ID A SELECT GROUP of prominent Americans meet in secret sessions between 1963 and 1966 and produce a report that advised the U.S. Government it could never afford an era of peace?

Yes—according to the mysterious new book, "Report From Iron Mountain on the Possibility and Desirability of Peace."

No—came a resounding chorus from worried Government officials, who, nonetheless, were double-checking with one another—just to make sure.

The response of experts and political observers ranged from "nutty" to "clever satire" to "sinister."

Is war necessary?

Central theme of the book, which purports to reflect the unanimous view of 15 of the nation's top scholars and

137

economists, is this: War and preparations for it are indispensable to world stability. Lasting peace is probably unattainable. And peace, even if it could be achieved, might not be in the best interests of society.

All this set off a blazing debate in early November, cries of "hoax"—and a "manhunt" for the author, or authors.

Sources close to the White House revealed that the Administration is alarmed. These sources say cables have gone to U.S. embassies, with stern instructions: Play down public discussion of "Iron Mountain"; emphasize that the book has no relation whatsoever to Government policy.

LBJ's reaction.

But nagging doubts lingered. One informed source confirmed that the "Special Study Group," as the book called it, was set up by a top official in the Kennedy Administration. The source added that the report was drafted and eventually submitted to President Johnson, who was said to have "hit the roof"—and then ordered that the report be bottled up for all time.

As the turmoil mounted, so did the speculation about those who participated in writing "Iron Mountain."

John Kenneth Galbraith, former Ambassador to India, was quoted by "The Harvard Crimson" as having parried the question of authorship.

Mr. Galbraith, who reviewed "Iron Mountain" under a pseudonym, was reported to have said: "I seem to be, on all matters, a natural object of suspicion." And he added: "Dean Rusk, Walt Rostow, even Robert Bowie could as easily have written the book as I. Yes, Rusk could."

Several sources turned toward Harvard in general as the site of authorship. One even went so far as to suggest

that the book is an effort by Kennedy forces to discredit
Lyndon Johnson.

A big spoof?

Whatever else it was, "Iron Mountain" raised fears at
high levels that it would be a mother lode for Communist
propagandists. There was also a feeling that if the book is
just an elaborate spoof, it is not likely to find understanding or sympathy in world capitals.

In the academic community, many held the view that
"Iron Mountain" was a hilarious hoax—a kind of dead-
pan parody of the studies emanating from the nation's
"think tanks."

One history professor at a large Midwestern university,
telephoned by "U.S. News & World Report," came on the
line with these words: "I didn't do it." But he added:
"Whoever did is laughing his sides off. He's saying, in
effect, 'Look, if you read and take seriously some of the
bilge in these exalted studies, you might as well read and
take seriously my little exercise.'"

In all the furor, a literary analogy cropped up. Not
since George Orwell's "1984" appeared some 18 years ago
has there been such a controversial satire.

"War is Peace"

Mr. Orwell's characters spoke a language called
"newspeak." They lived by the all-powerful state's slogan:
"War is Peace."

In "Report From Iron Mountain," the language is the
flat, metallic jargon dear to the U.S. bureaucrat. The message: War is, "in itself, the principal basis of organization
on which all modern societies are constructed."

Who Wrote It? A Fad In Political Comment Is Using Pseudonyms

Cryptic 'Iron Mountain' Book Is Written by a 'John Doe'; 'Americus' Criticizes LBJ
By Felix Kessler

The book is expensive for it's size ($5 and 109 pages) and the title sounds leaden: Report From Iron Mountain On the Possibility and Desirability of Peace. But it is a pre-publication sensation.

No wonder. Iron Mountain purports to be a high-level, once-secret Government study of war and peace. Its chilling conclusion is that continuation of war is "indispensable" to the stability of our society and possibly even to its survival.

But the real focus of controversy is the author—"John Doe." He is described as an eminent social scientist who was clandestinely recruited to serve on the special study commission. The writing is authoritatively bureaucratic but quietly preposterous as it concludes that an outbreak of peace would be disastrous.

The Guessing Game

Who is John Doe? John Kenneth Galbraith? Mr. Galbraith says no. Then is it Kenneth E. Boulding, the economics professor? He also denies authorship. Whether hoax, satire, or authentic, Mr. Doe's work is but the most recent in a wave of pseudonymous political commentary.

Iron Mountain implicitly takes to task all the nuclear planners and Doomsday thinkers. But much of the pseudonymous political writing has been sharply partisan. In the Oct. 28 issue of the New Republic, for instance, a "well-known historian" identified as Americus suggests hopefully that President Johnson could be defeated if dissident Democrats oppose him strongly and if Republicans run a candidate "attuned to the electorate."

Mr. Johnson is the target in the Sept. 16 issue of the New Yorker, where a writer with the pseudonym of Bailey Laird argues through a mythical Democratic leader called Daley Unruh that the President has little appeal to the average voter.

Much of the gossip in publishing would have it that Bailey Laird is Richard N. Goodwin, formerly a speechwriter for Mr. Johnson. But Mr. Goodwin says no. "I've denied that steadily," he complains. "But no one wants to believe it."

In fact, while others are speculating about Mr. Goodwin, he is busy pondering the identity of Americus. Could it be Arthur M. Schlesinger Jr., another former White House aide? "I doubt that it's Arthur," Mr. Goodwin decides. "He would have told me." Historian Eric Goldman, yet another erstwhile White House aide, is Mr. Goodwin's candidate.

The Man and the Name

Matching the man with the pseudonym—or ruling out contenders—is hazardous. For one thing, the disavowals tend to be ambiguous. Mr. Galbraith, former U.S. Ambassador to India and now a Harvard University professor, more or less denies that he wrote Iron Mountain. "Some things are so removed from reality that they can't be commented on," he says.

Mr. Goodwin is convinced that "anyone who thinks he has more freedom to write under a pseudonym is crazy, because that kind of secret can't be kept." And Harold Hayes, editor of Esquire magazine, adds, "Nothing is written that's so hot that it couldn't go under an author's own name."

Nonetheless, Esquire is publishing a 28,000-word excerpt of the pseudonymous Iron Mountain Report. "We think it's an important piece," Mr. Hayes says.

Publishing sources speedily recall that Mr. Galbraith had written pseudonymously for Esquire before, as Mark Epernay. And Mr. Galbraith reportedly is to write a book review of the Iron Mountain Report using the name Herschel McLandress.

Herschel McLandress is the fictional subject of the articles written by Mark Epernay. But, from behind an apparently impenetrable thicket of pseudonymity, Mr. Galbraith seems determined to evade the question of whether or not he authored the writings at issue.

"The only reason for using a pseudonym is to disguise one's identity," he says, accurately enough.

Dial Press, which will publish Iron Mountain Nov. 30, is running out 25,000 copies, a large initial printing for a specialized book. It contains a 20-page foreword by Leonard Lewin, a freelance writer who says he received the book from Mr. Doe and brought it to Dial.

For this Mr. Lewin is receiving all the author's royalties, according to Dial Press, but he denies being John Doe. (Mr. Lewin readily concedes, however, that he has used the pseudonym L. L. Case in the past for satirical articles.)

Political pseudonymity has a long, distinguished history. The most celebrated example in modern American times is the 1947 article proposing containment of the Soviet Union, written by George F. Kennan, then in the State Department, as Mr. X.

The magazine in which it appeared, Foreign Affairs, was called to account recently on the morality of disguising an author's identity. Foreign Affairs published an article about the Vietcong, identifying the author as George A. Carver Jr., a student of political theory and Asian affairs.

The magazine neglected to mention that Mr. Carver is employed by the Central Intelligence Agency. Sen. J. William Fulbright and historian Henry Steele Commager, among others, bitterly criticized this as an instance of unethical propagandizing by the CIA.

"I think we made a mistake," says Philip W. Quigg, managing editor of Foreign Affairs. "It would have been better to give him a pseudonym and let it go at that." Some critics say this would have been an even graver deception. (Mr. Quigg says the CIA was "adamant" in its refusal to have the author identified fully.)

Disguising a CIA man's identity, Mr. Commager says, is immoral because it would "fool readers into thinking the article is an honest, scholarly work." the only pseudonymity he condones is when a writer feels he must criticize his contemporaries or even close friends, and doesn't want to bruise personal feelings.

Some observers think the pseudonym is in vogue simply because people enjoy speculating who is eviscerating whom. One guessing game involved a critic of defense policy who withholds his identity but leaves no doubt about his convictions. He uses the pseudonym Raymond D. Senter (dissenter).

APPENDIX 6
NEW YORK TIMES
NOVEMBER 26, 1967

In Praise of War
By Robert Lekachman

WHAT IS AN EFFECTIVE VOICE of despair? The unusual answer offered by Leonard Lewin in this mini-bombshell of a book is the language of bureaucracy. Accordingly, he has created a bureaucratic fantasy, at least as plausible in its details and argument as Richard Rovere's celebrated revelation of the inner secrets of the American Establishment. Let us assume, Lewin instructs us, that the President appoints a highly secret, extremely prestigious study group, charged with the analysis of the consequences of transition from the semiwar economy of the 1960's to a truly peaceful world.

This Special Study Group, as it soon dubs itself, includes social scientist, natural scientists, an industrialist, even a literary critic. Although its initial opinions and prejudices are as varied as its members' backgrounds, the group decides early in its deliberations that it will examine its difficult assignment with as little reliance as possible upon either professional or personal preferences for peace or war. In the best American tradition its ethic will be severely empirical—it will seek to discover what peace will mean, and it will judge the merits of peace according to its practical consequences.

All of this is couched in the costive language of the public commission, conscientiously devoid of personal style or picturesque phrase. The manner is *echt* committee writ, the natural tone of a contemporary bureaucratic society. The group's conclusions disconcert its own members: there is no satisfactory substitute for a war economy. Only a war economy can furnish the minimum stability and coherence a society requires to survive. Lewin, a Hobbesian at heart, perceives the state as an organization whose *raison d'être* is defense against the foe, domestic and foreign. It follows that a statesman who is faced with a shortage of enemies will invent some. The prudent statesman best defends his society by attacking foreigners, ever careful, of course, to deploy the rhetoric of peace and pacification.

War, or at least preparation for war, is indispensable to social integration. More than that, "defense" expenditure is the only truly acceptable technique for the maintenance of reasonably high employment, satisfactory profits and suitable rewards for the engineers, experts and miscellaneous wizards who operate the levers of our technological economy. Hence in Lewin's judgment the long 81-month boom, which still continues, is a tribute much less to the conversion of American influentials to Keynesian economics than it is to the persistent escalation of military spending.

Within this context, Vietnam is a fine illustration of the ease of securing acceptance of any level of spending so long as it promotes certified military objectives, just as the sad fate of appropriations for Great Society programs amply demonstrates the grave inadequacy of social improvement as an outlet for surplus resources and idle men. And of course the Pentagon decision to finance a "thin" anti-ballistic missile system, soon, doubtless, to be succeeded by a plumper one, insures massive spending even if Vietnam phases out instead of escalates.

Are there really no substitutes for war? If we believe our guide, the answer is no, for the trouble with substitutes is their tendency to develop their own momentum. One cannot as readily regulate social as military spending. Almost any plausible, peaceful use of resources soon comes to be an expected part of the Gross National Product and therefore difficult to manipulate as an economic regulator. The space race is the best alternative to a war economy because the supply of planets and galaxies should suffice to allow practically perpetual and ever more expensive tooling-up for more and more grandiose missions. Even so the space economy is less satisfactory than the war economy because it contains less of an indispensable binding element, hostility to foreigners. Perhaps if we are lucky our space explorers will find hostile life on other planets.

Thus in the end Lewin's study group as honest men can only conclude that peace is far too expensive a state of affairs for responsible men seriously to contemplate. Is this no more than a bad dream Lewin has obligingly shared with us? If would be reassuring to say so. But without accepting every detail of the author's somber speculations, there is, I freely concede, a certain nasty plausibility about his conclusion. If we (and others) really cherished the values we so tediously articulate, among them world peace, elimination of poverty, racial inequality and social justice, why—the question will not stay down—do we find it so depressingly easy to fight wars and finance the Pentagon, and so exceedingly difficult to rebuild the cities, rehouse the poor and educate decently the nation's children? There must be something that as a society we get out of the values that we actually act out.

Lewin has chosen an apt form for the expression of an enormous pessimism about the drift of our society. It is a part of the grim joke of his book that he may only think that he has invented his study group. Such a group may in truth even now be working. One suspects that in the immediate aftermath of a nuclear war, committees will be creeping out of their shelters to assess the consequences of massive social folly.

The Guest Word
By Leonard Lewin

THE BOOK CAME OUT in November, 1967, and generated controversy as soon as it appeared. It purported to be the secret report of an anonymous "Special Study Group," set up, presumably at a very high level of government, to determine the consequences to American society of a "permanent" peace, and to draft a program to deal with them. Its conclusion seemed shocking.

This commission found: that even in the unlikely event that a lasting peace should prove "attainable," it would almost surely be undesirable; that the "war system" is essential to the functioning of a stable society; that until adequate replacement for it might be developed, wars and an "optimum" annual number of war deaths should be methodically planned and budgeted. And much more. Most of the Report deals with the "basic" functions of war (economic, political, sociological, ecological, etc.) and with possible substitutes to serve them, which were examined and found wanting. The text is preceded by my foreword, along with other background furnished by the "John Doe" who made the Report available.

The first question raised, of course, was that of its authenticity. But government spokesmen were oddly cautious in phrasing their denials, and for a short time, at

148

least in Washington, more speculation was addressed to the identity of the Group's members and of their sponsorship than to whether the Report was an actual quasi-official document. (The editors of Trans-action magazine, which ran an extensive round-up of opinion on the book, noted that government officials, as a class, were those most likely to accept it as the real thing.)

Eventually, however, in the absence of definitive confirmation either way, commentators tended to agree that it must be a political satire. In that case, who could have written it? Among the dozens of names mentioned, those of J.K. Galbraith and myself appeared most often, along with a mix of academics, politicians, think-tank drop-outs, and writers.

Most reviewers, relatively uncontaminated by overexposure to *real-politik*, were generous to what they saw as the author's intentions: to expose a kind of thinking in high places that was all too authentic, influential, and dangerous, and to stimulate more public discussion of some of the harder questions of war and peace. But those who felt their own oxen gored—who could identify themselves in some way with the government, the military, "systems analysis," the established order of power—were not. They attacked, variously, the substance of the Report; the competence of those who praised its effectiveness; and the motives of whomever they assigned the obloquy of authorship, often charging him with a disingenuous sympathy for the Report's point of view. The more important think-tankers, not unreasonably seeing the book as an indictment of their own collective moral sensibilities and intellectual pretensions, proffered literary as well as political judgments: very *bad* satire, declared Herman Kahn;

lacking in bite, wrote Henry Rowan, of Rand. Whoever wrote it is an idiot, said Henry Kissinger. A handful of far-right zealots and eccentrics predictably applauded the Report's conclusions.

That's as much background as I have room for, before destroying whatever residuum of suspense may still persist about the book's authorship. I wrote the "Report," all of it. (How it came about and who was privy to the plot I'll have to discuss elsewhere.) But why as a hoax?

What I intended was simply to pose the issues of war and peace in a *provocative* way. To deal with the essential absurdity of the fact that the war system, however much deplored, is nevertheless accepted as part of the necessary order of things. To caricature the bankruptcy of the think-tank mentality by pursuing its style of scientistic thinking to its logical ends. And perhaps, with luck, to extend the scope of public discussion of "peace planning" beyond its usual stodgy limits.

Several sympathetic critics of the book felt that the guessing-games it set off tended to deflect attention from those objectives, and thus to dilute its effects. To be sure. Yet if the "argument" of the Report had not been hyped up by its ambiguous authenticity—is it just possibly for real?—its serious implications wouldn't have been discussed either. At all. This may be brutal commentary on what it sometimes takes to get conspicuous exposure in the supermarket of political ideas, or it may only exemplify how an oblique approach may work when direct engagement fails. At any rate, the who-done-it aspect of the book was eventually superseded by sober critiques.

At this point it became clear that whatever surviving utility the Report might have, if any, would be as a point-of-departure book—for the questions it raises, not for the specious "answers" it purports to offer. And it seemed to me that unless a minimum of uncertainty about its origins could be sustained—i.e., so long as *I* didn't explicitly acknowledge writing it—its value as a model for this kind of "policy analysis" might soon be dissipated. So I continued to play the no-comment game.

Until now. The charade is over, whatever is left of it. For the satirical conceit of Iron Mountain, like so many others, has been overtaken by the political phenomena it attacked. I'm referring to those other documents—real ones, and verifiable—that have appeared in print. The Pentagon papers were not written by someone like me. Neither was the Defense Department's *Pax Americana* study (how to take over Latin America). Nor was the script of Mr. Kissinger's "Special Action Group," reported by Jack Anderson (how to help Pakistan against India while pretending to be neutral).

So far as I know, no one has challenged the authenticity of *these* examples of high-level strategic thinking. I believe a disinterested reader would agree that sections of them are as outrageous, morally and intellectually, as any of the Iron Mountain inventions. No, the revelations lay rather in the *style* of the reasoning—the profound cynicism, the contempt for public opinion. Some of the documents read like parodies of Iron Mountain, rather than the reverse.

These new developments may have helped fuel the debates the book continues to ignite, but they raised a new problem for me. It was that the balance of uncertainty about the book's authorship could "tilt," as Kissinger might say, the other way. (Was that Defense order for 5,000-odd paperbacks, some one might ask, really for routine distribution to overseas libraries—or was it for another more sinister purpose?) I'm glad my own Special Defense Contingency Plan included planting two nonexistent references in the book's footnotes to help me prove, if I ever have to, that the work is fictitious.